T0380289

A New Journey

MARY ANN TATE

WestBow
PRESS®
A DIVISION OF THOMAS NELSON
& ZONDERVAN

WestBow Press books may be ordered through booksellers or by contacting:

WestBow Press
A Division of Thomas Nelson & Zondervan
1663 Liberty Drive
Bloomington, IN 47403
www.westbowpress.com
1 (866) 928-1240

Scripture taken from the King James Version of the Bible.

ISBN: 978-1-9736-6803-9 (sc)
ISBN: 978-1-9736-6802-2 (e)

Print information available on the last page.

WestBow Press rev. date: 11/14/2019

From the author:

My thanks to Sandy Petty for being available to help with her computer skills and my son Mitchell Petty for proof reading and editing. Thanks to Joan Hart's suggestions with wording and structure and to her husband Roger M. Hart, author of "The Little House By The Edge Of The Woods," series who helped with editing and rewriting. Also, thanks to Debbie Dittenber for editing the final version.

Mitchell Petty

Prologue

Life's a journey, sometimes good and then at other times, not so good. Every person is unique just as each thumb print and snowflake are different. So are the actions and reactions in each of our journeys. The individuals or main characters in the five stories of this book illustrate my view.

The challenge, as you read through them is to discover both the physical and spiritual connection which bonds them together.

Enjoy 'The New Journey' of life.

Dedicated to my daughter Anne:

Anne

'A New Home'

Chapter One

Seattle, Washington

At first sight of what was to be her new home, Anne was overwhelmed and frightened by its enormous size. It wasn't just it's enormity that frightened her; it was dark, bleak and scary, scarier than the orphanage where she had been left as a baby. The small, cruel looking windows appeared cold and foreboding. They seemed to dare any sunlight to enter and brighten either itself or its occupants.

Something had certainly changed this part of God's green earth for there was none of its original beauty left. The isolated dark stone house sat in the midst of its ugly surroundings. Winter had stripped the maple trees of their green, red and orange colors. The only things left to bring life to this desolate part of the world were the scrubby Shumaker trees with their bright red leaves and the conifers with their somber hues of dark green. A winding stream lay ice bound and sterile white. The surrounding fields were brownish grey with patches of dirty snow. The weak sun was disappearing behind conifers leaving the house engulfed in a haze of foreboding mystery.

Anne experienced a powerful urge to flee to somewhere more inviting, surely there was someone who needed her in another part of the world. But having no other options at this time she paid the cab driver her fare, squared her shoulders, mentally chastised herself and bravely walked up the steps to the front door.

On her way Anne saw a small building setting apart from the main house making it even more isolated than the main house and wondered if it would be her living quarters. Even if it was small, she had never had a whole house to herself and thought it would bring a welcome change from the orphanage.

In an attempt to shake the mood of her surroundings, she mused jokingly,

"Wonder what the butler looks like, Dracula?"

She pushed the bell authoritatively and heard muted hollow sounds ring out, Bong, Bong, and Bong.

It seemed a long wait before the door began to open slowly and when it did, she first thought it opened itself. She gazed upward expecting to see a tall man and until she looked downward, she overlooked the dwarfish creature standing inside the door.

"Good grief," she thought. "It's a child."

But no, it definitely wasn't a child though its sex and age were hard to determine since it wore one of the weirdest outfits she had ever seen. The bright colors with their smooth satin finish seemed to mock the twisted body they clothed.

When Anne identified herself, the enigmatic creature drew back within itself and muttered,

"You're expected." Then turned abruptly and started moving away from her. Anne assumed she was to follow it and did so into a room like she had never seen before. Apprehension and anxiety filled her now as she was about to meet her new employer.

Anne was an orphan and after the death of her only relative, an uncle, she was without a home, armed with only a high school diploma and very little money. Her Uncle John located her just six months before his death and when he died, she was surprised to discover his bad investments had depleted all of his fortune.

She felt devastated but then fortunate when one of Uncle John's friends, and family manager Alan, arranged her this new position. After living fifteen years at the orphanage and then three years with the Shellynn family her Uncle John found her.

She felt indebted to the Shellynn family who took her in as a foster child until she finished high school. Out of gratitude and respect she started using their last name as her own. She had never formed any good or lasting friendships, so she was not unhappy learning her new place was located in Seattle, Washington, thousands of miles away. She felt lucky to not only have a job but also a home awaiting her. At the tender age of eighteen she was to begin a new adventure, a new life, but without God.

Her new life had led her to this mausoleum like building, following an unusual person down a long and dark hallway wide enough to accommodate the large double doors at the end. It paused seemingly to redistribute itself, knocked softly, and then struggled to open the massive doors.

The room was nothing like she had ever seen or imagined, it was huge and dimly lit, and shadows abounded everywhere. There were objects on the walls and even the ceiling had things hanging down. Still paradoxically a warm, bright and crackling fire danced under an ornate mantle. A large darkish cat sprang up arching and spitting out a welcome. A long thin arm appeared out of a highbacked chair and pressed the animal down into an uneasy silence. Then a presence rose up claiming the arm and Anne almost fainted.

The sound of "Good afternoon, Miss Shellynn" revived her.

"Oh, thank you," Anne whispered a prayer. "Its human."

She felt relief flood her entire being but a bit foolish as she stood facing a very slim and elegant lady. Her grey hair was upswept in a regal style crowning a face with soft lines lying serene over a bone structure which defied age. "She could be fifty or even seventy years old," Anne thought.

She considered curtsying when faced with such a queenly figure but instead reached out to shake her hand.

"Mrs. Vincent," she said timidly and without meaning to slightly bowed her head. She wouldn't have been surprised if the lady extended a golden scepter to touch her hand.

The grand lady said, "No, Mrs. Vincent is my mother."

Her reply stunned Anne, how could anyone so old have a mother. She couldn't respond and just stood there silently pleading for someone or something to help her out of this awkward moment. At her young age this lady looked like a grandmother herself, so Anne never expected to hear, "That's my mother." Fortunately, the butler appeared at that point and after being told the real Mrs. Vincent was not available to them, young Miss Vincent said,

"Darth will show you to your quarters, I'm sure you must be exhausted from your trip. I'll have one of the maids bring the evening meal to your room." With a great sense of relief Anne escaped the moment and followed this dwarf of a man up the long stairway.

Anne had arrived worn out after a long and tiring journey but full of anticipation for her new life she had set before herself. After Darth left her alone Anne stood silently staring out her bedroom window at the bleak surroundings. The view wasn't a beautiful landscape of conifers laden with new white snow. All she could see were the bare limbs of Maple, Elm and Birch trees stripped of their former beauty while clad with the green, red and orange leaves. The garden below appeared dark and uninviting without any of its summer beauty.

She sighed, "I wonder if this will ever seem like home?"

She hadn't stood at the window long before someone was knocking at her door. "Must be the maid with my supper," she thought. It was but Anne almost lost her appetite when she opened the door and saw a young girl with a twisted back holding out a tray but saying nothing.

"Did that old cat who welcomed me downstairs bite her tongue off?" Again, she silently wondered.

Shaking herself to stop staring she reached out and took the tray from the girl and thanked her. The poor young maid just nodded her head and walked away.

Chapter Two

*T*he next morning, Anne arose from her canopy covered bed feeling tired and disoriented after a long and restless night. Today was the first day of her new occupation as companion to Mrs. Vincent. Her duties seemed vague in the beginning, but poor Anne didn't feel she was in any position to be choosy. She felt fortunate to be offered anything and had jumped at the opportunity. She certainly didn't want to jeopardize it by asking too many questions. Now she wished she had!

When Anne heard the somber toned clock chime strike seven times, she shook off the empathy and began preparing for the day. This strange Darth had informed her the previous night that breakfast would be served promptly and only at 8:00 AM sharp. Evidently from his haughty manner she felt certain he didn't approve of the hired help being served in their rooms as she was the night before.

She really wasn't hungry but needed to get started on the right foot and that meant presenting oneself groomed and ready for the day beginning at breakfast time, eight o'clock sharp!

So, at five minutes to the hour Anne left her room and descended the long curving and ornate staircase. She turned left at the foot of the stairs and walked down the dimly lit hall to the entrance of the main dining room. Darth had informed her of its where-a-bouts and that she would take her meals with the family. Anne didn't know if it was an overture to make her comfortable with the family or an opportunity for the family to examine and judge her worthy of being with them.

She was speculating as to who or what construed the family as she opened one of the doors and entered the room. She stood facing a long table which was large enough to seat a small army. In fact, the walls surrounding it were lined with pictures of stern commanding figures.

"Ancestors, and quite a few of them," thought Anne. But she wondered how many living members were in this present army and more important, who was the commander in chief?

She glanced around the table and saw a little group seated together at one end. As she walked slowly toward them her eyes were drawn to the figure at the farthest end who was nearly engulfed in an overly large wheelchair. Still there was an aura around the figure which seemed to leave no doubt as to who was in charge.

This had to be Mrs. Vincent. The other members seemed to fade as Anne approached her seated grandly in that throne like wheelchair. The young girl felt drawn by an invincible force. Again, as the day before, she experienced the desire to turn and flee. But this time she couldn't even if she decided she must! This tiny, fragile appearing person was willing her to come.

Then a voice which clapped like thunder said, "Come here girl, don't dawdle, let me have a look at you!"

Anne stood as if thunderstruck. It took a few seconds for her to realize the voice, which sounded as if it came from the center of the universe, had in fact originated out of the mouth of that person seated in her throne like wheelchair. Upon viewing the body draped in white with its dry lined countenance, Anne thought, "It's a mummy. No. it's the mommy!"

"Miss Shellynn, Miss Shellynn," the sound struggled through to her consciousness, "Are you alright?" Anne's erratic brain succeeded in connecting with the voice.

"Oh yes, yes, I'm fine, sorry." The startled young girl stated.

"Would you care to take that seat?" inquired the old lady as she pointed a long bony finger toward an empty chair.

"Yes, thank you," answered Anne as she dropped into the designated chair.

After being seated she looked at the person to her left, a middle-aged man with a shiny bald head. He looked like a tubby Buddha except for his expression, rather than a serene smiling face he was scowling. Anne wondered if her presence was the reason for his frown. She smiled tentatively at him and he abruptly turned his back toward her. He spoke to the gentleman seated beside him;

"Sebastian, can you give me a lift into the city today? My car is in for repairs, and Darth has the day off."

The other one replied, "Sure Martin, be glad too."

Anne couldn't help staring at Sebastian; "Oh", she thought, "he's so handsome!"

He stood out like a jewel in the macabre setting of humanity. He looked as if he'd come from another planet. A virtual, huge blond shinning god! When he felt Anne's eyes on him and returned her look, she felt a sensation explode and flood throughout her body. Even her extremities were on fire. He smiled and nodded his head at her, and she felt as if she'd received a divine blessing.

"He's so gorgeous," she thought and returned his smile.

Young Anne was so flustered she felt she should say or do something in response to his gesture but could only manage a meek, "Hello." He seemed amused and this unnerved her even further. She turned away quickly looking straight ahead and tried to organize her thoughts.

Directly across the table sat Miss Vincent whom she'd met the night before. She asked Anne if she'd slept well. "If you only knew," Anne thought but instead answered, "Yes ma'am, I did. Thank you."

Anne wished she could think of something bright, witty or even amusing, to say. She wanted so much to get that man's attention! She'd never believed in that old cliché of 'love at first sight,' but after seeing Sebastian she felt he'd just made her a believer. She'd always been a cool, contained and somewhat calculating type, perhaps due to her upbringing and no one had ever made much of an impression on her. Nor would she ever have believed it possible to feel like a hormonal teenager, breathless and overwhelmed by his effect on her.

Striving to overcome her agitation Anne turned to the person at her right side. Unfortunately, she was in for another shock. That dining companion looked like an aberration from Hades! She unknowingly flustered out,

"First the beauty, and now the beast!"

Luckily for her, this creature of a man thought she said, "First beauty and now a feast." And in response, said,

"No, Miss, it's just the regular fare."

"It speaks," she thought. "I'm saved," and then sighed.

"Lesson number one, never be surprised at what or whom I see in this place." Her chagrin over the slip of tongue was soon overshadowed by the pitiful outcry of the old lady.

Everyone turned toward the sound and saw Mrs. Vincent frozen stiffly as she sat like a statue. One hand was holding a dish cover and the other clutched to her breast as she stared down at her plate. Lying on its bed of lettuce, surrounded by blood red tomato wedges, was a black and obviously dead bat! He was obviously dead and there was a small piece from a tree limb which someone had made the end of it pointed like an arrow.

A folded piece of paper was tucked under one of his wings. The members of the family quickly arose in unison and gathered like a protecting wall of bodies around the frail woman.

"Donald," she quivered, "What is that?" She pointed to the paper.

Her brother reached over and took it out of the bat wing, unfolded it and said;

"It's a note."

"What does it say?" she demanded. His poor scarred face appeared even more agonized as he seemed reluctant to reply. Finally, with visible effort, he replied;

"Maybe we should just save it for the police."

"No, no, I want to know, right now," she ordered him. After a very expectant pause, he proceeded to read it out loud.

"From one old bat to another, soon you'll be just like me!"

Mrs. Vincent didn't want the police involved but the family became so upset, she finally consented. They came immediately and after viewing the evidence their opinion was that it was a sick practical joke. So, after reassuring them and suggesting no one take it seriously, they left.

Chapter Three

*L*ater without having eaten any breakfast, Mrs. Vincent told Anne to come with her to the library where they could discuss her duties.

"The library?" she thought. And, in an attempt to set her mind at ease, she thought, "Well, it is a place of learning and with all the things I've already seen there's got to be plenty of books on about every subject in there!"

Eager to get on with her duties she complied by pushing Mrs. Vincent in her wheelchair to their destination, the most beautiful library anyone could imagine. She put her employer in the center of the room facing an ornate sofa where she sat down and prayed her face would look very eager to begin the lesson.

The first item was one the elderly lady seemed quite adamant about. She wanted to make it very clear she didn't feel she needed a companion. Only her family's constant harping made her finally give in and agree. But she could not emphasize it too strongly, she would not tolerate anyone hovering over her. She was a very private person and would not have any invasion of the privacy she had worked so hard for over the years, something she cherished as much as life itself.

"Really, young lady, I can't even imagine what your duties are to be, but evidently for peace in the family, we must think of something ourselves. Otherwise everyone will be fussing over me and trying to plan my days, probably for the rest of the time I have left on this earth. Just because Dr. Hangerman's operation failed five years ago confining me to this chair doesn't mean there are any problems with my mind. Still my family can't seem to comprehend my mind is sound as a dollar. If I am content with a companion these next few years I can hopefully be left alone from their interference. Just remember I am quite capable of taking care of myself and my affairs. Thus, if you don't become too intrusive, you will do! Do I make myself clear?"

"Yes Ma'am, and even though I am inexperienced, I feel I can become an asset and not a handicap."

"Oops," she thought to herself. "Did I have to use the word, handicap?"

Earlier during the breakfast conversation, she learned that Mrs. Vincent still kept her hand in the family business, even though it sounded as if her son, Martin, and grandson, Sebastian, along with her deceased husband's loyal manager, Alan, and family retainer, worked jointly together as a team and actually ran the business. However, there was still one with the major control and supreme authority and that was the wheelchair bound elderly Mrs. Vincent.

Anne also discovered that the small summerhouse

she spied yesterday from her window was actually where Mrs. Vincent spent half days conducting business, so she suggested she'd take her there and help settle her in and then leave. Anne would be in her room available where she could answer the telephone extension from Mrs. Vincent's summerhouse.

She could also bring lunches for them to share and after eating she could help Mrs. Vincent back to her room for her prescribed afternoon rest. Then during that time Anne would run errands or do any chore required of her.

The late afternoons and evenings could be planned in such a manner that Anne could earn her keep yet allow Mrs. Vincent the freedom she needed.

"I'm sure you'll think of something, Ma'am," said Anne.

Then having reached a tentative agreement they proceeded through the enclosed walkway leading to the summerhouse. Since her employer was expecting a visit from her doctor, Anne was given the morning off. They agreed it would be a good opportunity to explore her new home and particularly, the land it lay on. Mrs. Vincent said yesterday was not typical because even though it was wintertime, theirs were always mild. Indeed, it was the first time in thirty years it had gotten cold enough to freeze the river. And like the fluke it was, the temperature had already started climbing back up during the night and the warming morning sun had melted all the snow on the ground and broken up the thin layer of ice covering the water.

Anne was free until lunch time which Mrs. Vincent personally chose to eat at one o'clock. This meal was the informal one served and eaten anywhere one chose as most of the inhabitants were busy elsewhere during the daytime hours.

Thus, the young girl with an expectant step returned to the mansion for a wrap and then found her way outdoors where she experienced a wonderful surge of freedom. She strolled toward other buildings set a short distance from the summerhouse and the main house. Upon approaching the nearest one she noticed a corral attached to it.

"Horses," she thought. "Necessary for the genteel horsy set I've found myself roped into," and smiled at her pun.

She didn't ride but thought longingly of one who might even teach her. Anne was still young enough to think social levels could be bridged and in fact dreamed of a terribly exciting future here. Her half formed hopes even overrode the anxieties and uneasy moments, to say nothing of the shocks she'd already experienced in the short time she'd been here. All in less than twenty-four hours! She needed to come back to earth.

She entered the stable and nearly collided with someone, it was one of the breakfast company and not the one she was dreaming about. Instead it was the horribly disfigured man, the last one she'd wanted to meet in that dim interior.

She realized after her first shocking impression of him that he had been badly burned in an accidental fire, which she was to learn, had sadly also taken the lives of Sebastian's parents. He lived with scars covering his face and half of his scalp was completely void of hair as was his eye lids and brows. The tortured creature was none other than Mrs. Vincent's brother, one named Donald.

Now Anne realized he must be quite younger than his sister because he was clad in boots and gophers, obviously dressed and able to ride. A feat his sibling couldn't have done for years. He seemed quiet and calm at the table, so the jittery young girl felt safe enough, but it was hard to look at his face. Evidently, he was used to people avoiding a direct confrontation and seeming to sense her discomfort, he asked,

"Do you ride, Miss? We have some excellent mounts here, both English and Western."

She replied, "Oh, no, sir, I've never had the opportunity. But I think horses are beautiful."

"There goes my mouth again", she thought. "Why did I have to mention appearances!"

But he didn't seem to notice and said;

"Well now you do and perhaps someone here can teach you."

Anne wondered who he had in mind, hopefully he wouldn't volunteer. She thought, "I simply couldn't be comfortable with him. It will be hard enough at meals. Honestly, his face does put one off their feed even though it probably doesn't bother the horses!"

"Well", Anne said, "I've got to run." And then thought, "I'm even starting to think like a horse, run indeed. I'll be lucky if I can just walk out of here without putting my foot in it. Oh my, here I go again."

She excused herself and slipped out of the stable. She went quickly toward the second structure. It was much larger than the first, probably a barn but one thing for sure, she wasn't about to go into it. Hard telling what she'd find there. She did notice a stairway leading upward to a second story landing on one side of the building. The sloping roof had an immense skylight facing north.

Intuitively, she thought of a studio and wondered if one of the family was an artist. She remembered the long elegant hands of Miss Vincent and she could tell her mothers were the same at an earlier time. Paradoxically the tuba-like Martin had slim creative hands and even more surprising were Donald's; even with his scarred hands held the silverware with the flair of a maestro.

And she thought of the long tapering fingers of divine Sebastian which acted as an aphrodisiac to her. She shuddered at the mental picture of his hands flowing over her and wondered what mastery he could create on her! *Wow!* Anyway, she'd learned that Sebastian was the grandson so perhaps he inherited more than business acumen from the legend, Mr. Antonio Vincent. Maybe artistic looking hands were a family trait, it seemed to be the only connecting one as every one of them was totally different. Each an original in her young mind.

She walked on toward one side of the mansion which contained her bedroom window. She looked up and saw the sun reflected in it. It appeared to be winking at her.

She smiled, thinking what a difference a little sunshine made. Instead of forbidding as it was yesterday the huge structure seemed to be welcoming her. She felt drawn by it and wondered if the house possessed some unforeseen power.

Chapter Four

*T*he serene silence of the morning was suddenly rent by a scream that sounded as if it came from the summer house. Anne ran to the opened door and entered. The sight that greeted her rooted her feet to the spot. Mrs. Vincent was lying beside her overturned wheelchair. She was quivering as she pointed a shaking finger toward an arrow protruding from the wall directly in line with where her head should have been!

"Lucky for me," she explained after Anne helped her back into her up righted chair and soothed her into coherent speech.

"The doctor was late and since I didn't sleep well last night, I dozed off a bit but felt my glasses slip out of my hand. As I bent over to retrieve them, I heard this sharp twang. It startled me and the unexpected motion caused my chair to overturn."

"Thank God," said the poor shaken old woman.

Anne was reminded of the dead bat with its pierced eye! Now she knew it hadn't been just a practical joke! Some fiend had just tried to kill Mrs. Vincent the same way. Anne summoned her courage and went into the connecting room. There a door stood open to the outside. The young girl swallowed nervously and stepped through. To her relief, there was on one in sight! Relieved she returned to her employer and pushed her to the main house.

This time when the police responded, they had to admit they were wrong earlier. This was a serious matter! They were all business as they searched the summerhouse and its surroundings. After a thorough search they claimed to have found nothing except the arrow which was determined to come from a pistol type crossbow.

If possible, Mrs. Vincent's face became even paler than before. This news evidently shook her. One of the officers picked up on this immediately and asked, "What is it, Ma'am? Do you know who owns a weapon like that?"

She answered, "No, no, I'm afraid I don't. If you gentlemen would be kind enough to excuse me this has rather shaken me. I must go to my room and lie down."

Anne looked to the policemen and when they nodded yes, she wheeled the pitiful old lady to her bedroom. When they reached her room, Mrs. Vincent said; "Thank you dear, I can manage from here. I'll ring when I need you."

When Anne returned to the downstairs hallway, she found Donald with the police. They were in the process of telling him what happened. When they described the weapon, he was shocked even further.

"I've got one of those." he blurted out.

"You do?" they asked with interest.

"Yes", he said, "I use it sometimes to destroy rodents and other pests around her."

He said it was in the study with the family's gun collection and the younger officer asked him to get it.

He went for it but returned in a few moments looking puzzled.

"It's not there," he said. "I don't understand."

The police exchanged glances and then one asked, "Mr. Lee, would you mind telling us when you last used it?"

"I don't remember exactly, sometime last month, I think," he answered.

Then the other policeman asked, "Would you mind telling us where you were earlier today?"

Donald answered, "Well after I spoke with Miss Shellynn, I went for a short ride down by the river."

"Did you see anyone, any stranger, around the grounds, especially those close to the summerhouse?"

"No," he replied, "no one."

He seemed very upset as was evident in his jerky, erratic movements.

They thanked him and Anne, then left. When they were in the car, the youngest cop asked his partner what he thought about the whole thing and particularly,

"What about that guy? Isn't he something! He gives me the creeps! Quiet type but weird from what I've heard."

The older one answered, "Yeah, know what you mean; wouldn't surprise me if he tried to get rid of her.

But the big question is why? They've lived together for years without any problems that I know of. I understand he's alone a lot because he's an artist, who, according to the local art gallery owner, 'likes to create beauty in a beastly world.' Even though he's said to prefer his solitude, his sister insists he hang around, even to eating meals with the family."

"Man, I don't know, I don't think I'd have any appetite looking at that face. Ugh! Still with all that money and power, it wouldn't do the department any good if we started throwing accusations around. You'd need a truck load of evidence, to bring any one of them to trial. This town is mighty grateful, you might say even dependent on their good will because they own it! Without their business, there wouldn't be any town! And the taxes on that mansion must be unbelievable!"

Chapter Five

*T*he next few days passed without further problems and seemingly the police were at a dead end because nothing more was heard from them. Anne settled in and was content with her job. Also, Sebastian seemed to be interested in her and so she was happier than she'd been for a long time. Possibly more than any period of her life. He was even teaching her to ride.

As for the young man himself one couldn't phantom what was going on in his mind. He had a very suave and sophisticated demure. He displayed an old-world charm toward his grandmother. Yet to Anne, he was very modern in his mischievous and playful manner. Even though in his early thirties, he seemed as young as she. Except for the unguarded times when she observed him quietly, when he thought no one was watching, at these times he seemed distant and cold.

It made her apprehensive, but she closed her mind to those images she didn't really understand nor even want to. All she knew was she was crazy about him and wanted to be around him all the time. She would have been if she'd let herself, she was miserable when he was not near. Luckily, she had a lot of control of herself for a girl only eighteen years old. She had been shifted around all her young life until she ended with her Uncle John. She learned at an early age to lock up her emotions!

Still Anne's days flowed on and she had begun to relax when another unexpected incident shocked the family. They were again seated around the dining room table conversing in small talk. That is, except for Martin, who sat silently watching his mother toying with her food and feeding her old cat tidbits from her plate.

"I hate that cat," he thought and cursed. Suddenly Mrs. Vincent cried, "Tabitha, Tabitha, please someone help her."

They all jumped up to rush to her aid. The poor animal laid spread out on her back, eyes staring upward with its tongue protruding out the side of his gaping mouth. Unfortunately, Tabby was past any human help. It was quite evident the old cat was dead as a doornail!

They assumed she'd had a stroke. Even more surprising than her demise was Martin's offer to bury her. With that settled, Mrs. Vincent asked,

"Anne, will you kindly escort me to my room?" After she'd settled the elderly woman in bed Anne went downstairs to the kitchen where she asked the cook to heat some milk for her to take back to Mrs. Vincent, hoping the warm drink would settle her nerves and put her to sleep.

Meanwhile Martin, one not given to manual labor,

simply threw Tabby into the center of a bunch of leaves left in the wire enclosed incinerator. Then tossed a match into it and stood by brooding and watching the flames consume what he always felt was a blasted nuisance.

"Good riddance," he said. "You, stupid cat you were always underfoot and me tripping over you when I never expected it. Slinking and begging around the table. But worse yet were your eyes, waiting and watching. Well your vigil is over now and about ten years too late." He laughed and thought, "Don't cat lovers know if those sweet little pets were big enough, they'd eat you?"

The next morning Anne went into the bathroom that connected her bedroom with Mrs. Vincent's. Her first duty of the day was to wake Mrs. Vincent and assist her from bed to the specially equipped bath and dressing room. Then she would return to her room to dress allowing the old lady to bathe and dress herself with the aid of a unique mechanical system. When finished, Mrs. Vincent would call Anne and they would proceed to breakfast.

The routine was broken this time as Anne was unable to awaken her employer. She approached the bed where the old lady lay stretched out like a corpse. The girl was terrified she might be as dead as her cat! She was afraid to touch her and rang the bell to summon help.

Surprisingly Martin, whose bedroom was in another wing, was the first to appear. Running into the bedroom, he went directly to his mother's bedside and grabbed her. Shaking her he cried;

"Mother, Mother, wake up, please wake up."

The next person to show up on the scene was Sebastian. He put his arms around Martin trying to restrain him. "Get a hold of yourself man. What are you trying to do to Grandmother? Stop shaking her! Do you want to injure her? Stop!" he shouted.

He turned to Anne, "call Dr. Hangerman," he ordered, and she rushed to do his bidding.

She was able to reach the doctor at his home and quickly told him what was happening. He assessed the situation, and then told her,

"Miss Shellynn, I'll send an ambulance and will be there to meet it. Tell everyone to stay calm. That's the best thing they can do right now. I'll see you soon."

She returned to the family to give them his message, now completely represented in the group surrounding Mrs. Vincent's bed who still lay there motionless.

Chapter Six

*I*t seemed a long time before the ambulance arrived and transported Mrs. Vincent and her daughter to the hospital. Anne, Donald, Sebastian, and Martin followed in the family limousine.

They all sat together in the waiting room each lost in their own thoughts. The youngest one of the group was wondering if her life was about to change again? It all hinged on the old lady's recovery. Was she dead or alive? This was the unifying thought among them all, but of course for various reasons.

Finally, after what seemed eons of time, the good doctor came to speak to them. He seemed ill at ease, but his bedside manners were always bordering between evasiveness and downright rudeness. He seemed full of himself, opinionated and even tactless and cruel whenever it suited him. Worse yet, the majority of the family blamed his incompetence for putting old Mrs. Vincent in that wheelchair for life. At times, they even wondered about her competence as she insisted on being at his mercy, something they felt the good doctor lacked. Still they could not dismiss him. Only she could do that, if she was still able.

They rose rapidly at the sight of him.

"Is she alright? What's happened to her?" They asked. Everyone, with the exception of Martin, who seemed as though he couldn't care less, cried out with concern.

Dr. Hangerman answered, "Please sit down. Mrs. Vincent will have to stay for tests. I can't answer your questions until I get the results. At least you'll be happy to know I've managed to revive her. So, you might as well go home. It'll be several hours before I hear from the laboratory."

They agreed to go home after getting his promise that he would call them as soon as he knew anything! Sebastian thought, "If we live that long!"

The doctor called about three hours later saying he was on the way out to see them. When he arrived, the butler showed him into the library where Anne and the family awaited him. He seemed uncomfortable. He said they couldn't find any physical reason for Mrs. Vincent's coma like condition. Anne sensed his uneasiness and wondered what he wasn't telling them. Because she really didn't know him, she also wondered if that was his normal behavior, after all he was a member in the "brotherhood of silence." But he continued by saying Mrs. Vincent appeared to be fine now and completely recovered from her ordeal. Thus, if suitable arrangements could be made, he would be happy to have her released from the hospital. He did urge them to see that she had plenty of rest and said he'd stop by tomorrow to see how she was getting along.

After the good doctor left, they decided, knowing that she would prefer not to have her homecoming be a grand event, that only Anne and the chauffer would be dispatched for her. Also, they discussed the scanty medical report given to them by Dr. Hangerman. They were not happy to hear nothing could be found to explain the old lady's condition. Sebastian said he wished she had another physician, one who didn't appear to be the same age as his grandmother. In fact, he doubted his capabilities to assure anyone's physical wellbeing.

Martin haughtily replied that it really didn't matter what anyone there thought as his mother insisted on retaining Dr. Hangerman and obviously there was nothing to be done. He reminded them of how stubborn the old girl was, and in his way, imperialistically brought the meeting to a close.

So, Mrs. Vincent was brought home looking none the worse for her experience and said the sooner the whole escapade was forgotten, the better, she was fine!

As the days flowed by Anne became even more content with her job and began to believe she was fitting in quite well with the family. They all seemed to accept her. Really most of them were pleasant to be with after one got used to living in their mausoleum type home with its unorthodox servants. In addition to the dwarfish butler with his flamboyant attire and attitude, was the mammoth size cook, Mrs. Wilson.

She ran the kitchen like 'Attila the Hun', and engaged in a never-ending power struggle with rapier thin and steely Miss Dorothy, the housekeeper. Miss Dorothy dominated the daily help like a boot camp drill sergeant and even ordered Darth and the half deaf combination gardener and handyman, Mr. Wilson (none other than the husband of big mama, the cook) around and about their duties. And had living quarters in the basement.

Anne wondered if Martin locked them up at night and let them out in the morning. Martin seemed unable to get his life under control. She concluded from the comments of others that his various business ventures over the years had ended in failure. His parents always supported and encouraged him and finally he'd been drawn into the family business where he appeared to find his niche.

But as far as his personal life, that was another story. His attitude concerning people was not benevolent of his Buddha appearance. He was a controller with a superior attitude who seemed to prefer his own company over any others. No wonder there wasn't a younger Mrs. Vincent. Who could he elevate to his high level of expectations? When in reality, who would lower herself to the realm of his narrow, smug and small world? But all in all, he didn't find Anne offensive and seemed to tolerate the young girl fairly well.

Old Mrs. Vincent treated Anne kindly but with a quiet reserve discouraging the intimate relationship her optimistic young companion might have hoped for. Still Anne's nature was one of watchfulness and caution. That in itself could have spared the two of them a habitual closeness, one that might prove to be uncomfortable in the future. So, they seemed quite satisfied with each other just the way they were.

There was one small procedure that neither party liked but had accepted. After settling the old lady in her bed and before retiring herself, Anne would make sure the two doors of the bathroom connecting the bedrooms were left ajar. Even though Mrs. Vincent had a bell to summon help the family needed more reassurance and the time Anne found her in that coma like state didn't help any. Therefore, they insisted that in the likelihood she couldn't reach or even ring the bell, with the door opened, Anne should be able to hear any disturbance that was occurring in her employer's room.

But another, almost tragic, incident would soon make both parties appreciate what had seemed unnecessary in the beginning.

Chapter Seven

One night something disturbed Anne's sleep and she awoke with a start! As she lay there in bed listening for Mrs. Vincent she wondered;

"What awakened me? Did I hear something?"

She couldn't decide as everything seemed normal. There wasn't any sound except the quietly gentle ticking of the clock. Still something had awakened her.

"Was I dreaming?" she questioned herself. She laid there, ears straining for sound, eyes straining for sight in her dark bedroom lit only by moonlight. The strongest sense, her nose, caused her to spring up to a sitting position. She turned on the bedside lamp. Smoke, she smelled smoke! And there appeared to be a light glowing under Mrs. Vincent's side of the bathroom door.

As the frightened young girl looked wildly around the room, she detected small wisps of smoke coming from Mrs. Vincent's side of the bathroom door. Glad she had left her door to the bathroom open, jumped from her bed and ran into the bathroom. Grabbed the handle of Mrs. Vincent's door and threw it open only to be met by the sight of flames!

Luckily, she was discerning enough to slam the door shut and then run to her door which led to the hallway calling for help. She hurried to Mrs. Vincent's other door and desperately tried to open it but found she couldn't, it was locked inside!

The first person to come to her assistance was Sebastian. She was surprised to see him. He had been gone for the past two weeks on a business trip and wasn't expected back till the end of the next week. Yet here he was running down the hall toward Anne and oddly enough considering the lateness of the hour, he was dressed in street clothes, a charcoal suit. However, the frightened girl's concern for old Mrs. Vincent didn't allow her to sense the significance of his appearance.

Sebastian tried the door only to verify what Anne already knew. It was dead bolted. By that time others were coming on the scene and they too were alarmed at the smell of smoke.

Miss Vincent called out, "Mother, Mother. Oh Mother! Please! Can't someone do something?"

Sebastian started shoving against the door and finally managed to force it open. The left side of the room was engulfed in flames. And worse yet tongues of fire were licking and leaping like a live thing, eating their way up the side and foot of the bed almost completely encircling the prone body of Mrs. Vincent. She looked like a sacrificial victim lying on an altar, an offering to the king of Hades! Sebastian saw this and jumped through the doorway and across the room through the fire spreading over the carpet. His grandmother was oddly not making a sound as her family cried out to her. He plucked her off the bed out of the mouth of the encroaching fire. Reaching down with one hand he grabbed her robe from the bed to cover her with. Then ran back across the room and slammed through the doorway with the old lady safe in his arms.

At that moment Darth raced past them with a fire extinguisher to battle the fire and Sebastian shouted to Martin, "Call the fire department. Anne, come help me with Grandmother!"

"Take her to my room Sebastian." said Miss Vincent and hurried to lead the way. After lying her down on the bed he began rubbing her hands only to find a piece of paper in one of them tightly quenched into a ball. He took it and was about to throw it into the wastebasket by the bed, but his aunt stopped him.

"What did you take from her hand," she asked?

He shrugged and then placed it on the bedside table. At that moment Mrs. Vincent began to stir and moan softly. Anne and Sebastian watched anxiously as her crinkly wrinkled eyelids fluttered open. Then Miss Vincent approached the bed murmuring quietly, "Mother, can you hear me?"

"Of course, I can hear you, girl. I can even see you! What is it?" But before her daughter could reply, the old lady began to cough. She coughed vehemently, so her frail small body threatened to fall apart. Anne and Sebastian helped her set up hoping to ease the burden on her fragile chest. Evidently, she was suffering from smoke inhalation. Her daughter suggested they call an ambulance and take her to the hospital.

"Nonsense, the old lady managed to mutter. If you would all give me a chance to catch my breath, and please open a window, then step back from me, I'd be alright."

To substantiate this, it appeared to Anne, Mrs. Vincent started to stand up, but Sebastian gently took her by the shoulders and held her down. While Anne's mouth dropped open no one else seemed surprised at her movement.

"Grandmother, please just rest a minute. Maybe you're convinced you are alright, but I'm not. You've had a close call. You have to take it easy. Just for a moment, please."

"Yes Mrs. Vincent, Anne concurred. We all need to regroup. Thank God you feel as well as you do. I, for one, am still in shock. I don't know what I'd do if…"

At that moment, Miss Vincent interrupted Anne by speaking rather abruptly, at least by her standard voice range, "Sebastian, we can tend to Mother's needs, why don't you attend to your own?"

Surprised by his aunt's uncommon rebuttal, he seemed to become aware of himself and rudely, halfway smiled to the ladies.

"I guess you're right." He looked at his image in the vanity mirror and saw a grey ghost like a washed out 'Christy Minstrel' with flashing white eyes and brilliant teeth.

"Sebastian," Mrs. Vincent said, "Forget about me, what about the fire?" Soon she was able to set up but continued coughing. She appeared to have almost been overcome by the smoke. While her daughter wanted to call the doctor her mother said, "No," she was more concerned about the fire.

"I completely forgot about it!" exclaimed Sebastian.

At the same moment came a knock on the bedroom door from a very black, soot covered Darth.

"Excuse me", he said, "I just wanted to let you know I've got the fire put out."

Unfortunately, the fire department was needlessly coming with their sirens wailing in the night. Sebastian tried to send them away when they arrived, but they refused to go.

"The chief always demands a written report, he said. He'll especially want an investigation into the probable cause," he went on to explain.

At this Sebastian showed them to Mrs. Vincent's bedroom where the fire started. The left side of the carpet, plus the bed, was completely destroyed.

After their investigation the firemen asked,

"Does Mrs. Vincent smoke?"

No one could answer his question.

Chapter Eight

*T*he fire chief came by later in the morning when all of the family could be present. He informed them the fire had started from a cigarette which had dropped on the bedspread. Apparently, and luckily, Mrs. Vincent had kicked the bedspread to the floor where it ignited the carpet.

Fire then spread to the door connecting her room and the bathroom blocking Anne from entering her bedroom. Fire was also on the floor leading to the hallway door, the only other entrance. Sebastian had no choice but to leap thru the fire to rescue his grandmother.

When the chief asked Mrs. Vincent if she smoked, she answered, "Absolutely not!"

The rest of them all looked at Sebastian as he was the only known smoker among the family and the help. But then he had just returned home and came in when Anne screamed for help. Of course, none of them volunteered his habit to the chief. It didn't help matters either when he informed them, he would have to notify the police.

"Nonsense", said Mrs. Vincent, "there's no harm

38

done, not even an insurance claim will be made. It was just a bit of carelessness which we are perfectly capable of handling ourselves."

"Now please Chief, let's just forget it; would you have a drink and tell us about that wonderful grandson of yours? How is he doing up at State? Our football team is certainly suffering from losing him. Who would have thought one player could influence the whole team. They aren't going to make the playoffs this year, are they?"

He replied, "I'm afraid not Mrs. Vincent, but as much as I'd like to stay and talk about Bruce, I've got to get back to the station. I guess we can let the incident go this time but please take my advice and be more careful. You were lucky this time, but you might not be again."

Sebastian thanked him and proceeded to walk him to the front door. In the meantime, Miss Vincent suddenly arose and went to her mother's burnt out room. She returned shortly to the rest of the family and with a perplexed expression said;

"I just remembered that piece of paper mother had clutched in her hand."

"What are you talking about?" demanded Mrs. Vincent but when her daughter unrolled the ball of paper her face became very pale.

"What it is, I say, what's the matter with you, Elizabeth?"

Sebastian took the paper from her and read it aloud,

"You've run out of lives, you old cat! Join Tabby in his fiery Hades."

After the note was read Mrs. Vincent instructed Anne to take her to the guest room, "This instant," she demanded! The young girl jumped to do her bidding while the rest of them stood silently by, obviously deep in their own thoughts.

When Anne, with the help of the housekeeper, had Mrs. Vincent settled in the bed, and Miss Dorothy had left the room Anne asked if she might speak with her for just a few minutes.

"Well, all right if it's important," she replied.

Anne knelt down beside the bed and said,

"Mrs. Vincent, even though I've only been here a few months, I've become quite fond of you and I just can't keep quiet about what's been happening to you. Obviously, someone is trying to hurt you, or worse. And yet no one is doing anything but pretending nothing is happening. I know how you value your privacy but please, Mrs. Vincent, call in someone to help."

In spite of the detached look on the old lady's face, Anne hurried on. "If you don't want the police and the publicity then hire an investigator, or detective, or somebody, please," pleaded the distraught young girl.

"My dear girl, I'm touched by your concern. But there are matters so involved that you are unaware of and I am not at liberty, nor do I desire to enlighten or worse, involve you. I also realize how frightening all of this has been, but you must trust me! I know what I'm doing! Now, dear, please leave me. I am tired and I wish to be alone," replied Mrs. Vincent as she dismissed the young helpless and somewhat hopeless girl.

Anne, while not reassured or pleased by the conversation, had no recourse but to leave and bid her employer goodnight.

It took some time, and quite a little effort, to clean and then air the smoky odor from Mrs. Vincent's room. In the meantime, she continued to sleep in the guest bedroom that was some distance from Anne's room. And again, this caused no little stir among the family members who finally surrendered to the will of their leader.

When everything returned to normal, they all seemed to put the incidents behind them. Sebastian continued teaching and teasing Anne in his spare time. And she, in her youthful enthusiasm, began to look forward to each day and was a sense of delight to most of them. Even Donald seemed captivated by her, in fact, paid her the ultimate compliment. He asked her to pose for him. He invited her to his studio, an unheard-of-thing which astounded the whole family. Anne was embarrassed and thanked him but declined. Sebastian teased her about that too.

He said, "What's wrong Anne? First you refuse to allow me to take snapshots and now even refuse an unheard-of-invite from Uncle Donald? Do you realize none of the rest of us have ever seen his studio and he certainly hasn't shown us any of his work? Now he says he wants to paint you! I don't think you realize how attractive you are, or you'd be throwing yourself in front of us."

41

"I'm sorry Sebastian, but I just don't like my picture taken and while I'm very flattered, I just can't do it."

Both Donald and Sebastian thought she was somewhat troubled and overreacting about something other than posing for her picture and couldn't help but wonder why?

Chapter Nine

*A*fter the fire, when all the cleaning, painting and refurbishing was completed, the days settled back into the usual routine. Mrs. Vincent spent the mornings in the summerhouse and early afternoons napping in her bedroom. On Tuesdays and Thursdays, she received visitors, and then on Mondays and Wednesdays Darth took her into town; occasionally on Fridays as well.

They were a strange combination on those outings. The butler sitting high in his post as chauffeur with a special designed seat and hand controls. The old lady in her white eastern country attire sat behind him in a special made electric wheelchair. The vehicle even had a lift which picked her and the 'town going' chair up and out on the sidewalk. The townspeople just shook their heads at her extravagance and wished they had her money.

She complained about so many things including that chair. She claimed the old chair she used at home was much more comfortable, yet her family knew she loved the independence and freedom of the motorized one.

She was a familiar sight whisking around to the bank, drug store, even the hardware store.

It was on a Friday, the 13th and Mrs. Vincent was going into town. Anne knew she needed some supplies and at the last moment asked Mrs. Vincent if she might accompany her.

"Of course, and do you remember what I told you about the big sale in that new department store and the specials at the drug store?" Mrs. Vincent asked her. What she didn't know was how lucky she would be on this unlucky day. In fact, Mrs. Vincent would owe her young companion quite a bit before the day was over.

Darth, combination butler and chauffer seemed surprised when Anne came out of the mansion with Mrs. Vincent. Then after helping seat her Anne went around to the other side of the automobile, opened the rear door and also entered. That is if surprise was the emotion which appeared briefly on his usually forlorn expressive face, then he entered the car.

The day was beautiful, and both of the women were enjoying the ride until the vehicle began acting strangely. After Darth swerved widely around the next curve Mrs. Vincent spoke sharply into the intercom,

"Darth, what on earth are you doing?"

He cried out, "Something's wrong with the brakes! The car is out of control!"

It was gaining speed as they were on a steep downhill slope. Then as they rounded a corner the road changed slightly and seemed to slow them down but abruptly the driver's door flew open and Darth, along with his seat, was ejected through it!

Mrs. Vincent sat rooted to the seat as if she'd turned to stone! Anne too was white as a sheet yet, thank God for the agility of her youthful mind and body. She sprang out of her seat and slid herself through the small sliding glass opening which separated them from the driver. She turned the motor off and grabbed the emergency brake. Even with Darth in his seat he would have been sitting too high to reach the handle. The brake held and she pulled off the road to a stop.

No longer terrified, the old lady couldn't stop praising her. Anne laughed, kind of shaky and said,

"Mrs. Vincent, please don't give me too much credit, thank the producers of that show we watched a few weeks ago, remember. The car's brakes failed yet the driver was able to stop using his emergency brake. I was so frightened, but we should be thankful for the television set too. I don't know if I'd been able to even think to do that if I hadn't seen the show."

"Well, as my late husband who was a very intelligent businessman used to say, 'don't sell yourself short'. And I have complete faith in your ability to handle an emergency. Besides, being of the female gender, you wouldn't want to miss a good sale," laughed her employer and sometimes, friend.

"But we do need to find Darth," she said.

Anne started the engine and slowly drove them into town using the rugged berm of the road to enable them to creep into town where she pulled into a gas station.

She went inside and called Sebastian telling him what happened and of her concern for Darth. She didn't know if she should call the police or an ambulance or if he would do it.

"You know how grandmother feels about the police," he answered. "I'll go look for Darth and his condition will determine the next step. There's a garage right next to where you are. Leave the car with them and they'll give you both a ride in their company van. The wheelchair will fit into it. And Anne, I'm glad you are both ok. See you later."

"All right," replied Anne feeling warmth from his voice.

They followed his instructions and one of the garage repairmen drove them home. When they neared the spot where Darth was ejected Mrs. Vincent told the mechanic to slow the car hoping to see Darth or his car seat but didn't see either one. They were becoming quite concerned about Darth but then Mrs. Vincent said something that shocked Anne.

"I never thought he'd leave me this way."

Anne was about to ask her what she meant but as they were approaching the mansion, she saw Sebastian assisting a dirty and ragged little person out of his car. It was Darth and his driving seat!

Then Anne, with the help of the serviceman, got Mrs. Vincent out of the van. She dismissed the driver and with Anne's assistance went over to see Darth who didn't seem too badly hurt. For Darth, he was moving around as usual but shamefully said;

"Mrs. Vincent, please forgive me. I don't know what happened. First the brakes wouldn't respond, then the door flew open and the next thing I knew I was flying through the air. I guess I was lucky, because of the training I had when I was young, I knew how to absorb the fall."

Anne seemed perplexed at his response, so Mrs. Vincent explained; he was an acrobat with the circus when my husband met him. He hired him after Darth's wife, a trapeze artist, died from an accident. Darth was so emotionally broken he refused to stay with the circus and has been with us ever since.

Then Mrs. Vincent kind of shook her head and replied, "My dear Darth, please, no apology is necessary. This mishap was simply a mechanical failure and certainly not one of yours. We're just thankful no one was seriously hurt, except for your condition, of course. But since none of your bones appear to be broken, might I suggest you have my grandson help you to your room and perhaps we should call Dr. Hangerman to come see to you?"

Darth hurriedly said, "No," and reassured his employer. "Please, Mrs. Vincent, there is no need to bother the good doctor!"

As a vision of the man flashed through his mind, Darth shuddered.

He thought, "I was fortunate to survive the fall, but I don't know if I could be lucky twice in one day, like lucky enough to survive the doctor. If his inaptness didn't kill me, his bedside manner would. I wish Mrs.

Vincent would get a real physician," Darth couldn't help thinking.

Later that evening after Anne had assisted Mrs. Vincent to her room and settled her in bed, she stepped outside for a breath of fresh air before returning to her own room. She was surprised to see something on her bed. On closer inspection she discovered it was a child's doll, a version of the old nursery rhyme character, Humpty Dumpty. Under his arm was a note. Anne picked it up, opened it and read;

"You survived the ride in the car,
And didn't go over the edge too far.
Maybe you should have walked on down
Don't ask for a ride again to shop in town"

The next morning Anne gave the doll with its macabre message to Mrs. Vincent who took it, read the note, and then told her to forget it, murmuring something about foolishness. Anne didn't want to antagonize her so she remained silent, hoping in desperation, nothing else would happen.

Chapter Ten

As if in response to the young girl's plea, there weren't any more incidents as time moved on. Mrs. Vincent seemed in good spirits and really Anne felt fortunate as the old lady was an undemanding and comfortable companion to be with. In fact, she didn't feel like 'hired help', she felt like family.

The only shadow in her existence was the increasing time Sebastian spent away from the house. Even on weekends he was constantly called to the telephone. After a Sunday afternoon of such interruptions Mrs. Vincent remarked on it saying it reminded her of the late Mr. Vincent.

She said, "I suppose that's why I became involved in the organization."

Anne couldn't help wondering how that decision affected her children. Martin and Elizabeth seemed rather cowed and in awe of their mother. Anne also wondered how Mr. Vincent's involvement in that huge conglomerate affected them. At the present time there certainly didn't seem to be much bonding between the three.

Still their children certainly weren't deprived of any material comforts. One had only to look around to see the opulent lifestyle available to them. To take a meal with them was a culinary delight, even the food was rich! And their automobiles, clothing attire, jewelry, even their haughty countenance spoke of inherited wealth and position.

According to Donald, he and his sister came from a long and very illustrious family. The ancestors lining the walls everywhere were evidence of continuing generations above the norm and proof of a prosperity which allowed history to repeat itself over and over. Only the wealthy seemed to be able to afford the respect and glorification of great-great-grand-grand.

Yet from small hints, innuendos of the hired help, Anne suspected Mr. Vincent might not have come from the same social register that produced Mrs. Vincent. Maybe he was 'new money'. Interestingly when one looked, most of the portraits, staring ahead, yet reflecting on the past, were of Mrs. Vincent's lineage.

Still if the siblings were aware of their mixed heritage, they didn't show it. Anne's first impression of Elizabeth Vincent was that of royalty. She looked, moved and spoke as a queen or at least a princess! Even Donald, in spite of his horrendous scarred face and head, carried himself as 'Lord of the Manor' and his bearing spoke of wealth and breeding.

Thus, the young girl was having her first experience in aristocratic circles. She sometimes felt like a hybrid version of Cinderella and Lisa Doolittle all wrapped up in youth and inexperience. She couldn't wait for the finished, complete, beautiful butterfly to emerge.

Sometimes she felt ready to explode, out of her shell, into what? That she didn't know.

Lately Miss Vincent had been excusing herself directly after dinner instead of joining the family in the library for the coffee and tea ritual preceded over by Mrs. Vincent. The daughter seemed, if possible, even more subdued than usual. Upon being questioned about her break in the routine she murmured something about selecting items from the attic for an upcoming auction for some charity.

Evidently her mother wasn't satisfied with the excuses for her absence because one evening shortly thereafter she also bid them an early goodnight. When Anne rose to follow, she put up a restraining hand saying,

"No, don't come with me. I have something to do and I am not ready for bed. I will ring for you when I am."

"Yes, Ma'am," Anne replied and watched as Mrs. Vincent wheeled herself out. She continued down the hallway to her lift. It was installed for her personally and no one dared use it as she declared it off limits to all. She reasoned to herself, "Don't they have perfectly good legs to carry them anywhere they wanted to go?"

"And everyone knows climbing stairs is wonderful exercise for the cardiovascular system!"

As the rest of the family was gathered around the

fireplace enjoying a quiet and serene repast, they were abruptly torn from their peace by a sharp scream that rent the air. They rushed out of the library and followed the sound of sobbing. They turned a corner and came upon a strange and disturbing sight, old Mrs. Vincent lying on the floor crying. Behind her was yet another weird sight, her wheelchair sat jammed between her elevator doors being held tightly as in a giant vise.

After they managed to extract the chair and set Mrs. Vincent back into it, she calmed down enough to explain what happened. It seemed she'd been on her way to see what her daughter was involved in. She was concerned about her behavior. Knowing her like she did, with her moods, she realized something was bothering her and it was more serious than just gathering items for charity.

She believed, although she didn't speak her thoughts out loud, that Elizabeth, in searching the attic for contributable objects, had come across memorable items that had been packed away years ago. Ones dealing with a suitor who rejected her literally at the altar.

Also, she knew Elizabeth had been using her lift because she had discovered one of her earrings on the floor just that morning. She was going to catch her in the act. Maybe it was a small thing to others, but old Mrs. Vincent knew matters could get out of hand if she used a slack hand to run a ship, a home, or a business. Thus, she decided to find out what her daughter was up too.

After explaining about her concern for Elizabeth, she proceeded to tell them what happened and how she ended up on the floor. It seemed that she pushed the button to the elevator and the doors opened allowing her to turn her chair around and back into the lift. When the chair's wheels entered the lift, she felt her chair tipping back and luckily for her she had the insight to throw herself forward out of the chair because the floor of the lift was still two stories down!

She further declared, "I will certainly call the company who made this elevator for me and have them come out and fix it! But in the meantime, I want every one of you to erase this stupidity from your minds, and above all else, do not and I mean, do not tell anyone, most of all Elizabeth! I'll handle her myself. Do I make myself clear?"

Then turning to Anne ordered, "Take me to my room as this chair seems able to function alright and goodnight to the rest of you."

The next day the elevator was repaired, and things seemed normal again except Mrs. Vincent had another plan for catching her daughter. That evening at the dinner table she informed the family that she was taking Anne to a musical at the theater. Everyone seemed a bit surprised as this was not a normal thing for her and wondered how attached she was getting with the girl? Still it was her business, not theirs.

The two of them dressed to go out and soon Darth came back informing his boss the vehicle was at the front door and ready. After they were settled in Darth proceeded to drive down the road. But they had only gone a few miles when Mrs. Vincent looked at her watch and told Darth to turn the car around, they were going back to the house.

Anne, of course was disappointed but she knew better than to ask any questions, assuming her employer-friend was not feeling up to the occasion. When Darth helped them out of the vehicle, Mrs. Vincent handed him a short list of things she wanted him to pick up for her at the drugstore. Again, Anne was surprised when she saw Sebastian also drive up, stop and get out of his car. He was supposed to have been out of town again.

Evidently Mrs. Vincent wasn't because she said, "Good, Sebastian, come with us, I want to show you something."

So, they went inside and down the hallway stopping at the elevator. She put her finger to her mouth silencing her companions. They stood there for a short while and Anne looked at Sebastian bewildered but he just shook his head and grinned at her. Then they heard the elevator descending and Miss Vincent, who was using the lift illegally, was caught red handed as its doors opened and she stepped through to see three pairs of eyes staring at her.

"What, what's the matter, Mother?" she stuttered.

A very angry matriarch was on the verge of telling her when Anne interrupted.

"What's that?" pointing at a white piece of paper lying on the floor behind the surprised Elizabeth.

Sebastian gingerly stepped in and retrieved the paper, opened it and read aloud. It said;

"You escaped the shaft of the bat.
You escaped the fate of the cat.
You escaped the runaway car.
Oh, the luck you've had so far.
But now you're splattered all over the floor.
I ask, can we expect any more?"

This time the shocked and shaken old lady did not protest nor stop a very troubled and determined family! They called the police.

Chapter Eleven

*T*he police arrived a short time later and were shown, once again, to the library where everyone except Mrs. Vincent, awaited. She had told Sabastian to inform the police about the life threating incidents then was taken to her room as she was expecting Dr. Hangerman.

It was an indication of her near collapse in this war of nerves being played on her by some unknown cruel opponent for an undisclosed victory or gain.

But by now everyone had to face the truth. There was someone among them bent on murder and most foul, on a frail old lady. They'd experienced the 'how and when' but not the 'who and why!'

The police had one clue. They knew most crimes were all connected by what could be gained. Therefore, the big question, 'who' had the most to gain from Mrs. Vincent's death? Find that person and they would prevent the crime, if they could do it in time. It was evident by the notes the perpetrator thought he, or she, was clever. Maybe he was just insane, hopefully not, because that might blow the 'murder for gain' theory apart.

When the police heard of all the attempts that had been covered up, they were not amused. This 'sweep the dirt under the rug' attitude only hindered any attempt to stop the crime. Maybe gave the criminal an edge, "If at first you don't succeed, try, try again."

Regardless, if the police could find out 'who' would profit the most from Mrs. Vincent's death, the case would be closed, and the 'why' prevented.

Unfortunately for this theory, upon questioning the family attorney, they discovered that everyone, including the servants, even Anne, would benefit financially from the old lady's demise. Yet even knowing who would gain the most might not give them the perpetrator. Some criminals would murder for a cup of coffee. Greed has no boundaries. What looks like a fortune to some may be a pittance for others.

So really the police were no further ahead in figuring out which one, or ones, were getting eager for their share of the family fortune. Thus, even though they hated to admit it, the police were stumped. And no one, not one person, came forth with any information. Also questioning them was like going against a wall. The aristocrats simply couldn't overcome their heritage, one simply didn't 'air the family's garbage' and the paid employees wouldn't 'foul their nests.'

Finally, after useless meetings with everyone living in the mansion, the score was, 'Criminals 5, Police 0.' As bad as they hated to admit defeat the police licked their wounds and slunk out.

The family and servants were left to settle into an

uneasy calm. They realized they all were suspects, worse yet, not only in the eyes of the law, but with each other, what had been a peaceful home was now entirely something different.

No one seemed to have much of anything to say to the others, in fact they all seemed nervous and thus an unnatural stillness lingered on. They each held an uneasy feeling as each wondered about the other one and time dragged on through the day.

But one thing very apparent to everyone was their concern for poor Mrs. Vincent. The strain was evident on all, especially on the intended victim. She seemed literally to be running down. No energy, no opinions, no orders, no desires, and no will. This ninety-year-old clock was about to stop ticking.

Then early one morning, the waiting and the suspense was over! The housekeeper, poor Miss Dorothy, found Mrs. Vincent lying at the bottom of the stairs with her wheelchair tipped over on top of her. Her head was at a strange angle and she was definitely 'very dead.'

The diabolical deed was done; this old cat had run out of lives.

Chapter Twelve

*T*he police were called, and everyone endured their questions again. Anne, who was the last one to see her alive, told them she had settled Mrs. Vincent in her bed for the night. No one had seen her after that. No one knew why she'd gotten out of her bed, or why she'd left her room. But the one thing everyone knew was, she was now dead! Also, the police were at a 'dead end'. Much to their dismay the police feared this would be another unsolved murder case. Shrouded in a family of secrets with no one willing to reveal the murderer's identity to the public. Mrs. Vincent had been one of, if not the most, important person in the community. Now, all the police could do was give the family their condolences and leave.

Later during the inquest, a startling discovery was revealed. It seemed that when the housekeeper and daily cleaning lady were in the summerhouse cleaning and gathering up Mrs. Vincent's personal items, they made an amazing discovery! The maid was polishing an old desk and she, as far as they could figure out must have accidentally triggered a release when a hidden drawer came out. In it was a book. "And what a book it turned out to be, definitely a top seller!"

A diary, one might even say a confessional diary. But truly amazing was its contents. Miss Dorothy, and righteously so, took it to the police. After all the things they had seen they were, and rightfully so, the most surprised of anyone.

Mrs. Vincent exposed her true self, a devilish and cunning schemer! All the incidents involving the attempts on her life were the results of her own hands!

The old lady seemingly was in a quandary and perhaps felt the 'ends justified the means.' She didn't know who could fill the major and immense responsibility of managing and controlling the vast Vincent Empire. She had helped the late Mr. Vincent, who had inherited it from his father, as it continued to grow. Their monument to immortality. It was a grave decision and she could not fail.

She proceeded to create situations in which each prospective member could be tested. These, of course, family participants were her brother Donald, son Martin, grandson Sebastian, even seemingly the last chance, was given to daughter Elizabeth. She'd hoped their handling of the pressures of the drastic situations would or could be construed as a barometer of their potentiality as director of Vincent Enterprises.

Ironically, she even put poor young Anne to the test. She was still irritated the family had made her hire her but then she rationalized that Anne didn't have to take the job, period! She also knew that the innocent, caring girl just might get in the way of her schemes.

Still paradoxically, she wanted their reaction to her personal danger. Even though the practical, smart business sense demanded the capable leader, perversely she thought, "ability isn't everything. This person will literally be the heart of our empire and he or she better have one. They have to be able to feel the lifeblood my husband and I pumped into this, to realize it was our life. I will not tolerate some coldhearted piece of humanity to profit from my death!"

There was another side of her too which no one ever suspected. She had a sense of humor. She was quite capable of walking, in fact, walked most nights enjoying the sounds of the creaking of the old floors which added to the many times people, including family said the place was haunted.

She was also clever enough to know when and where to go and nobody ever discovered anything, that is until her dairy was found. Guess she wasn't as smart as she thought but one thing for sure, she was very creative. She demonstrated in every incident and her conclusion of each how very insightful and clever she was. She would have probably made more money as an actress.

Chapter Thirteen

She started with incident number one with the dead bat that was to simply set the stage for the rest. No one else was to be involved. Of course, one thing did stand out, the family all showed their concern for her.

She wrote, "Goodness, I didn't realize that part of me existed, I rather enjoyed being the center of attention."

Incident two was her testing of Donald. It left no doubt of his love for her. Anyone with half his eyes could see he was devastated. In fact, too much to be in control of the family concerns. The only good thing was he came out of his shell a bit more and seemed to make an effort to be more congenial, even offering to open his studio to Anne when he asked her to pose for him. Mrs. Vincent also had a key to his studio; one he never knew about. It was one of her favorite places to visit on her night journeys. She was amazed at the paintings and sculptures he created. They were so beautiful portraying beauty in an ugly world. He was a genius who hid behind his art. She shook her head knowing the world would never know it till his death. And sadly, was not a candidate for the business world.

Incident number three involved Martin, who was the only living son and naturally the obvious inheritor of the Vincent Empire. Unfortunately, both his father and mother spoiled him, and it wasn't until he reached adulthood, they realized how much. Mrs. Vincent knew full well of his failures in past ventures. Yet he was extremely intelligent, a bit ruthless with a bulldog tenancy. Thus, he would do if he could rise above or change certain characteristics. As of now he was his own worst enemy.

She was sad but smart enough to know she needed to move on, she certainly would not have her heart dictate the destruction of the Vincent legacy. An interesting footnote to this incident was how Mrs. Vincent used the veterinarian report to justify her action. It seems he told her Tabitha had a cancer, fast spreading, yet very painful. He wanted to put Tabitha down immediately. Mrs. Vincent said she needed time to think. Cleverly she decided she could use this in her quest. She knew the gardener kept rat poison which contained potassium cyanide and would put the poor cat out of her misery very quickly. She put it in her food and fed the tidbits to her pet. As demonstrated, the old lady could be ruthless if necessary.

Incident number four was Sebastian's test. He was the only offspring of the oldest son who, along with his wife, were killed in a tragic automobile accident leaving Sebastian to be raised by his grandparents. Mrs.

Vincent knew Mr. Vincent was grooming him for an important part in their organization. In fact, he, with the help of his grandfather's old manager ran most of the business, of course under Mrs. Vincent's authority. But she was afraid of the time period missing from his life. Between the age of twenty-one and twenty-five she discovered he had been a mercenary and was afraid there might be something that could come back and hurt or destroy the family name, or the business. After two years he still disappeared for short periods.

Still the fire showed Sebastian could act fast in an emergency. It also revealed he was willing to risk self for Mrs. Vincent's welfare. And he was cool under fire from the police. He was even more concerned about her now with all that was happening. In fact, so much that she was still concerned about the secret closed inside of him.

But she was encouraged by his interest in young Anne, she too was an unknown ingredient, therefore Mrs. Vincent wanted to test her in the next incident.

Incident number five involved Anne and the limousine. It was the first time she decided to take a risk, one which could have cost her life. While watching a movie on the television with Anne that showed an episode involving a runaway limo almost identical to hers, she hatched the idea to use it herself. She took another chance by involving Darth. He cut the brake line. She also planted the idea of shopping into Anne's mind. Luckily the young girl did not panic. Mrs. Vincent hadn't any backup, but then she had always been a pretty good judge of one's character. It was only concerning this vast project that truly tested her talent. Actually, she was involved too closely, and it was throwing her off.

Still she was impressed with Anne. Also, every incident seemed to be drawing Sebastian and Anne closer. Yet she felt compelled to dig further back in Anne's past. There were unanswered questions. They really didn't know that much about Anne's past. She hired someone to check her out but unfortunately when he asked for a picture Mrs. Vincent told him how camera-shy she was. She also mentioned Anne refusing to allow her portrait to be done but she said she could handle it.

The final incident number six involved her daughter Elizabeth and the lift. As expected, when she was seen by the family exiting from the elevator, one she wasn't supposed to be in and with another vicious note on the lift with her, she was obviously taken back. Yet she immediately regained her composure and showing little emotion seemed more concerned about the suspicion of the police than the possibility of her mother's demise. Mrs. Vincent also noted that Elizabeth headed more charity organizations and ran more benefit programs than a dozen women would handle. Under that shy, mild decorum was a precise, efficient, clever mind, very like her late father. But she lacked his, for lack of a better word, humaneness. She was more concerned about public opinion than the near tragedy of her mother's incident. Thus Mrs. Vincent eliminated her as a possible successor.

Fortunately, or unfortunately, it all depends on how one looks at it, with her death came an end to the diary, to the turmoil caused by her, and perhaps to a dynasty.

But her death raised even more questions, one in particular, was that she had been night walking and tripped, or was she pushed along with her chair? And if she was pushed, by whom? They didn't find among her belongings any will because there wasn't any. It was on this quest that she was trying to make up her mind who was to get what, mainly the control of the Vincent Empire, unfortunately her demise ended this. All the family had to go on was the late Mr. Vincent's will. He had given the business and control of his share of the money to Mrs. Vincent. The house was to his daughter, Elizabeth, with the provision, his wife and existing members were to have lifetime residence. Upon the occasion of Mrs. Vincent's death, the business jointly would go to Miss Vincent and Martin. Fortunately, they were both out of town on the night of her 'accident.'

The following week, the family was notified by their attorney, Mr. Rightling that he needed to meet with them and what a shocker it was! It seemed his father who had been Mr. Vincent's attorney had messed up terribly. Or was it his mess or act of divine intervention? In the process of cleaning up after Mrs. Vincent's death an old safe was found. Inside of it were old records and one of them was an addendum to his client's will. To honor Mr. Vincent's deceased son, he gave everything to his only heir, Sebastian!

Another surprise, and almost as staggering to the

mind as the first one; the day after the amazing find Sebastian asked Anne to stay and be his wife. If Anne accepted she would become the new Mrs. Vincent of the Vincent Empire.....

Dedicated to my nephew Terry Lee

Terry Lee

'A New Treasure'

Chapter One

California, Rocky Mountains

*I*t was a cold blustery day and the wind howled angrily around the log cabin. Terry Lee sat up in his bed trying to decide what he needed or wanted to do. He really didn't need anything but what did he want, that was the question? He had plenty of wood for the fireplace and cook stove, plenty of food supplies unless he acquired a craving for some fresh meat. Still there was plenty of deer in his smokehouse. And if he wanted to, he might bake some bread or biscuits.

The thought of biscuits baking in the oven brought memories of home in Indiana flooding to his mind and he wondered what his mother, Jane, was doing. He had left what remained of his family behind in Indiana to go see the western mountains. That was what he started out wanting but now he wondered about his decision, it did get lonely with no one to talk to.

The only essential thing was water and there was plenty just outside the door even though it was in the form of white fluffy snow. So, having all his necessary provisions he really could do about anything he wanted with the day. "*Heaven forbid,*" as his mother would say. He might just stay in bed.

"Ah, the pleasures of winter and solitude," he thought.

Unfortunately, cabin fever set in and he became restless. The thing he liked about the cabin, at times like these, was also what he didn't like. Another of his mother's sayings was, "Too much of a good thing is what makes the cream go sour."

And today he longed for more room to move around and someone to talk to. With the dark wooden floor and walls becoming a bit depressing he decided to go tend to his dogs. Days like these made him wonder if he had made the right move coming to and settling on this mountain.

This seemed to be one of those days so the only alternative to brooding about his past was to boot up and get out. Well, at least long enough to feed his husky friends living outside in their body warmed house. He could've kept them inside with him, but he never was able to get used to the noise and then of course they hadn't had a bath in months because of the cold weather.

Also, he couldn't stand it when they had gas. No way was he going to put up with their stink. But, on the plus side they were warm bodies and someone to talk to. He thought it was unfortunate they couldn't talk back, or was it?

Man, he hated to argue, that was one of the reasons he liked it up here in the mountains. Peace, oh the bliss of peace and quiet, especially after he married that troublesome woman last year.

"Well, that's what you get, he thought, getting drunk and marrying that bar girl. What was her name?" He and others called her a lot of different names.

He had another regret tugging at his heart for pulling up his drawers and getting out of her space without divorcing her legally. He wondered if she'd still be down there in town when he went for supplies in the spring.

Blast it all, she had to work in the best place in town. Excuse me Lord, guess I should've said second best.

Outside of weddings and funerals he didn't have much fun attending church. But then the wine wasn't bad, it made communion more interesting.

Still he communicated every day with the Power he felt was greater than himself in his neighborhood. And not just asking for better hunting or weather. He did appreciate all he had and thanked the Lord lots of times. He had to laugh when he remembered thanking Him that the bullet didn't ricochet when he missed a deer.

And when he came upon that bear cub and its mama tried to come after him. Now there was a day to write home about. Then there was the avalanche that just missed him snuggled up in his nest behind a boulder.

Oh yeah, he thanked Him a lot that time. Seemed like all his life he'd been in the wrong place at the wrong time. Trouble just seemed to follow him.

After seeing to his four-footed, friends Terry went back inside his cabin to hibernate the rest of the day. But the peaceful bliss he looked forward to, was suddenly interrupted when he heard a pounding on the door.

Then a man's voice called, "You in there, Terry Lee?"

So much for peace and quiet he thought, getting out of bed again and grabbing his pants to pull on over his long johns.

"Just a dad burned minute," he yelled.

He opened the door to find two people standing there and speak of the devil, here she was, his bride along with one the locals.

Oh mannnnn, he thought, trouble just come knocking.

He wanted to slam the door and lock it! But then decided it wouldn't be the right thing to do. Later he realized sometimes the right thing turned out to be the wrong thing. Oh well he was kind of young and time did have a way of teaching a man a few things if you were lucky enough to have enough of it.

So, he said to them, "Come on in."

The local man Terry knew as Jim, was a good hunter but a bad poker player. Also, he couldn't hold his liquor, but he sure was holding onto that girl as she tried to struggle out of her heavy coat.

Terry tried to think. What's her name, oh yeah, Lula Belle, yeah, that was her name, Lula Belle, how could I forget that?

We had an ole' mare by that name when I was a little kid. Had to shoot her though she bucked Pa off and broke her leg after running away. Shame though cuz she was a pretty thing. Lula Belle, must be something about that name.

Oh well Pa wasn't hurt, only his pride and what he sat on. The next week he had to eat most of his meals standing up or laying down.

Chapter Two

*T*ad was Terry's nick name, short for tadpole, which was what his Pa always called him. It helped him get a sense of humor because he had to laugh whenever he thought of or heard the word 'frog'. The name seemed right because his Ma always had him hopping around doing chores.

And that's how he acted when his Pa used the strap on him whenever he got into trouble which seemed like a lot of times. And growing up hadn't helped him much. Guess that was another good excuse for living out of harm's reach isolated here in the mountains of good old California.

He couldn't understand how some poor unfortunates preferred the ocean. Man, it never settled down much and talk about not making up your mind, it just comes in and out, back and forth, back and forth. And then think about what lives or lurks in it. Sharks with teeth so sharp they could tear coral apart, but then again if they didn't really eat them the salt in the water might preserve them, he didn't know.

He wondered if that was why those old Loch Ness

creatures lived so long. And talk about anti-social there are those barracudas, they'd bite a big chunk out of you given the chance. And what about those jelly fish, they hurt being the little guy trying to keep up with the big guys. Of course, they can't, so they just sting you bad with their tails. That's funny because they ain't even big enough to bite you. Terry had a good friend who liked the ocean, and he wouldn't hurt anyone. He got stung by one of them on his ankle and almost lost his foot. After that he lost his courage and lives by himself in a cave somewhere.

What a pity, well anyway, Tad lost his tongue that fateful morning as he stood there looking at his company wondering which one of them would find theirs or have the guts to just use it.

Jim found his first. "Sorry Tad, I didn't know anywhere else to take her and she did ask me to bring her up here."

Jim looked down at the floor and said, "I ain't been so lucky with them cards and I needed the money. She said she'd give me some to bring her up here."

Then she spoke up, "Tad, I'm really sorry but do you have a few extra dollars for Jim?"

"Oh man, here you are, and you don't have any money. Why are you even here?"

"I just needed to get away a few days," she said.

"Get away from what," he asked. "You bad at cards too? Did you kind of get caught cheating, Lula Belle?"

She laughed and Tad really didn't even know she had a sense of humor. Truthfully, he didn't know and didn't want to know much about her. When he married her, he was drunk and just wanted a woman's company but now he wished he'd never even met her. If not for marrying her he'd have thrown her out of his cabin. Later he had plenty of reason to think he should have done it, but so much for hindsight.

As they huddled around his stove trying to get warm Tad spoke out, "If you'll give me some room, I'll heat up some coffee for you."

They moved over a bit for him to put the pot on. "Are you hungry?" he asked. His good manners came from his Ma. Ole' Jim spoke up, "Iff'n it ain't too much trouble Tad, I am a little hungry?"

Guess he learned that from his Ma too, being polite, I mean. Don't know who taught him the bad ones, his Pa or old life?

"Well, I just happened to have some leftover soup setting on the back of the stove and some leftover bread, kind of dried out," he explained but then thought feeding them this stuff wasn't too much trouble. Anyway, he was getting kind of tired of that soup as he'd been eating it for three days.

Well, he told them to take a seat and he'd dish them up some soup. After they sat at the table and started eating, there was that heavenly sound. Quiet came into his place again as they scarfed the food down like they were starved. Or maybe just tired of beef jerky, beings as it takes a couple of days to get here from town. And cooking over a campfire didn't seem too easy for town folks. They get kind of spoiled and forget how to live out on the trail. Tad thought that applied to ole Jim's hunting spells too, easier to go into the general store and buy what he wanted. Course those poker tables seemed to be robbing him of eating money.

Chapter Three

After they finished eating, Tad went after them again.

"So, what brings you here?" he asked.

The girl stared at the floor and thought,

You already know why I'm here but answered,

"I didn't have anywhere else to go."

"So why did you have to go somewhere?" He asked curious to find out why she had to move now.

"Someone I knew from the past came looking for me."

Another husband, he prayed to himself. Then I wouldn't be married to her.

He knew that much about the law and just thinking of the law he asked her if it was another husband or some other trouble.

"No, I don't have another husband," she replied. "Nor did I do anything bad. I was just in the wrong place at the wrong time."

Haven't I heard that before, Terry thought.

Sober, you can't fool me much.

Next, she added, "I only need a place to stay till

he leaves town. I don't think he saw me, so it probably won't be but just a few days."

Terry moaned, hoping it was only for a few days.

Jim, being warm and well fed, had drifted away, but suddenly he woke up and said,

"Well, I guess I better be gettin' back, course after you pay me."

"I don't have any money, will a skin or two help you any?" Terry asked.

Terry thought, that if Jim didn't want to be skinned himself, he didn't have any other choice. Jim nodded his approval and took the two skins Terry gave him that were decorating the wall, then hurried out. Terry wondered why Jim wanted to leave his warm cabin so soon, but he didn't ask.

Terry thought he lived by the rules of a Christian man or he would have made Lula Belle leave with Jim, but he didn't. So, he decided to spend the rest of the day outside. He checked his traps down by the frozen river and found nothing. After resetting the ones that needed it, he trudged around his winter wonderland marveling at the peace and quiet.

Toward evening he was getting cold and hungry. Yeah, it would probably have to be leftover soup for dinner. Otherwise, he would have to fix something because he didn't really expect the girl to even know how to cook. She sure could dance though. Maybe she'd dance for her supper. Ha!

"How's your day been?" he asked her.

She didn't say anything but handed him a bowl of

soup and looked at him as if he'd said something stupid. Was she smirking or was that her way of smiling? After a couple of warm relaxing hours, he suggested they turn in. He gave her his bunk and stretched out by the fireplace. Should've been the reverse, didn't cats like to sleep by the fireplace?

Now that was funny, he thought, but she probably wouldn't have liked to hear it.

The next few days passed pretty much like the first day, Tad stayed outside most of the daylight hours with his dogs and ran his traps. A few raccoons and an occasional mink were found in his traps, but most of their food had been taken out of the streams, years ago.

His mind wasn't really on trapping, but how to get rid of Lula Belle. He couldn't think of an easy way to get her out of the house and felt trapped. She wasn't even pretending like she intended to leave any time soon.

During the fifth night a noise woke Tad and he went to the window where he pulled the flour sack curtain aside to look out. It was pitch black except for a slight moonlit spot showing snow being tossed around.

Was it the wind howlin' or the dogs I heard, he wondered? Something didn't feel right, so he started to open the door only to have it slam him back onto the floor.

Wow, that's some wind, he thought except it wasn't the wind!

Something was in the doorway. He hoped it wasn't another mama bear.

"Get out! Get away!" He yelled.

But a voice bellowed back, whose voice he didn't know, so it couldn't be Jim coming back. Anyway, Jim wouldn't be acting like this. In an instant he knew it wasn't Jim and scrambled toward the fireplace to get a candle. From the candlelight, he could see an intruder pointing a gun at him.

"Who are you and what are you doin here?" He yelled while trying to stay calm.

The man bellowed in a deep, gurgley, scratchy voice, "Juss sshut up and sset down."

By this time, sleeping beauty was awake and said in a quivering voice, "Can I get up?"

"Yeah, Lucy, you can get up," he snarled out. "And get a lantern lit!"

"Ok", she murmured submissively. She passed Terry like a ghost and took a lantern off the fireplace mantel and managed to set it aglow. As the room began to light up, the man looked around and said,

"Cozy little place you got here Lucy. It took me a couple years, but I finally found you, didn't I? Knew I would, and I've done it."

"Lucy", Tad exclaimed! "You told me to call you Lula."

He looked at Lucy and the intruder,

"Who are you anyway?" He asked both of them.

"Never you mind who I am," the man growled and that left little doubt in Tad's mind that he wouldn't be a welcome guest.

"I met your friend Jim in town at the bar. He seemed

to know about everybody in town, so I asked him iff'n he'd seen this bar dancer. He told me that he had in fact, last week. She'd asked him if he knew of someone that she could stay with that lived kinda secluded. He told Lucy where you lived, Tad," and then laughed at his good fortune showing yellowed teeth from years of chewing tobacco.

"And then Jim said he heard you was a nice guy and would probably enjoy some company livin' out here alone surrounded by a forest of trees and high up on this mountain. He agreed to bring her up here and told her about the clothes she'd need to wear and supplies they'd need. Lucy told him she was broke," and then the intruder laughed again thinking about what she had taken from him. Tad couldn't help wondering what the big joke was about.

"Lucky for her, unlucky for him. He somehow he'd manage to scrape up what they'd need," the intruder with the gun explained.

Tad thought poor old Jim probably met this unnamed man in town and now he's left in a pile of snow someplace down the mountain.

Tad decided he was better off to play along with this stranger.

"How can I help you?" he asked.

He knew it sounded foolish to ask if he could help this man, but it did help break the man's attention away from waving his gun.

It drew a loud response and he laughed really hard at Tad's question.

"Oh yeah," he barked, "You can help me, sshut up! Now Lucy, stir up that fire and let's get more comfy."

He kind of halfway smiled as he looked at her so Tad felt a little better. Obviously, Lula or Lucy didn't, because she looked scared. But she did get more logs from beside the fireplace and threw them in. That was better, more heat and light.

"Why'd you run away from me, Lucy? Not even a goodbye kiss. I gotta admit you surprised me. I thought we had a good thing goin'. Didn't we?"

"Yes, we did," she murmured.

"So, I ask you again, for the last time, why did you leave me?"

Tad was starting to get kind of curious himself. Why did he track her down and why the gun? A lover's quarrel or did she steal somethin' from him? Or did she get him drunk and married too?

He just had to know, never could mind his own business, but then again, legally she was his business. Also, this was his home and this stranger was rapidly becoming an unwanted guest. He was also starting to get mad. Still, he respected the gun being pointed at him and he didn't want to get shot. So, he tried to defuse the situation and asked him what he could call him? The man sneered at him like he'd just crawled out of a hole,

"You can call me Boss."

"Well then Boss, can I get you something to drink?" He had a jug of moonshine that was powerful stuff and thought it might change his attitude or at least get him to lay down that gun. When Tad showed him the jug, Boss said, "Ok that looks good."

So, Tad poured him a large cupful which he drank, then poured it full again. So far so good, Tad thought and offered one to Lucy thinking a drink might help settle her nerves too, but it didn't. Her nervousness wasn't helping any, but she took the cup of moonshine and sat down across from Boss then Boss motioned with the gun and told Terry to sit down beside her.

Chapter Four

*O*utside the wind grew louder as the storm raged on. Snow swirled and beat on the cabin until Tad couldn't hear himself think due to the noise. Conversation was nil between the three inside, but Tad didn't mind as he tried to think of a way to get rid of Boss. Boss seemed to be thinking too, and drinking. Tad was wishing the storm had delayed Boss's arrival for a day or two because now it seemed he was stuck with Boss and Lucy. For how long, only Mother Nature knew.

Boss seemed in a dilemma like he didn't know what to do next. Tad couldn't help wondering what did happen between Boss and Lucy. He wanted to know, but in a way, didn't want to know. Finally, Boss started talking to her about two of his buddies that she evidently knew. He said they missed her too and wondered where she'd gone.

Then she started talking and said she'd grown tired of the place and didn't think it really mattered to anyone if she was to leave. She wanted a new start and when a trucker told her about our town, which was his destination, and said she was welcome to go along. So, she did.

Lucy told Boss, "I thought it was too good of an opportunity to miss. The trucker was anxious to get started as he had a lot of freight to deliver and was already way behind schedule. So, if I was to go it had to be right then. I'm awful sorry Boss, but you and your crew were out of town so I couldn't tell you about the trip."

"But," she said quickly, "I left a letter for you with the bartender which told you where I'd be."

"Really," he said sarcastically his gravelly voice gurgling with the effect of moonshine.

"Guess the man lost it," she explained.

"And you got lost pretty good too. It's taken a lot of drivin' and lookin' cause that trucker had a lot of stops to make but you left a trail. That red hair with its widow's peak is kinda hard to forget. Plus, that little thing-of-ma-gig by your lip. Kind of like a dot on a map and I knew where you would probably be hanging out."

Boss continued, "Then I got to this little town only to find out I lost you again. But the luck of the draw was with me playing with old Jim. His luck suddenly got better and took two five-dollar bills off me. Course, he was cheated when he got paid only two ragged furs from you. So, I decided to let him keep the money and hire him to bring me up here. It took most of the day and it was evening time when your cabin finally come into view. Jim told me since I wouldn't need him anymore, he'd just hightail it back to town. He reached out and shook my hand then turned around to leave. Unfortunately, he didn't see me turn around too, and follow him a short distant. I hit him over the head with a big rock that I found, and he fell to the ground. Then I robbed him of my fee and the few extra coins he'd managed not to lose in his search for riches. I dragged him off the trail and buried him under the snow and some broken tree limbs."

"We parted company right back there in that bunch of redwoods. Don't think he'll be missin' my coins unless he's playin' with the devil. Ha, ha, ha."

That fired Tad up. Ole' Jim wasn't much but his life still mattered. He'd miss him! He definitely wouldn't miss this good-for-nothing man who was looking tired or just whiskey relaxed.

Tad was getting ready to jump Boss but guessed he must have sensed something, 'cause he took down a piece of rope from the rafter, gave it to Miss Lucy and made her tie Tad to the chair. After checking her knots, he told her to get into Tad's battered steamer trunk. He slammed the two sides together and locked it. Flipped it over and tucked it tightly in the corner by the bunk bed where he laid down and went out like a light.

Tad tried his best to wiggle loose but couldn't. He tried scooting his chair toward the door, but it made a scraping noise that woke Boss up. Boss came off that bed and hit him with his gun and that's the last thing he saw.

Guess he needed the sleep because it was daylight

when he woke up. His head hurt so bad he thought he was the one with a hangover.

Boss let the girl out of the trunk. She didn't look too good and moved like an old woman. He told her to build the fire up and cook him something to eat. Guess the soup was all gone. She produced some eggs. Tad wondered where she found them, unless maybe she and Jim had brought some delicacies with them.

"Man, I'm starving," Tad said to Boss. "My stomach is growling something fierce."

But his guest wasn't sharing. Boss did let him open the door so he could relieve himself. He didn't like what he saw though. That storm was still raging and had already dumped about three feet of snow. It didn't look like anyone was going anywhere for a while and none of them were happy about that.

He was tied back up to that chair again and Lucy, after going outside to use the potty can, huddled in the corner. Boss got the luxury of the bed again with the jug of 'feel good'. The moonshine wasn't doing its job, because it never did knock him out.

Then later that afternoon Boss said,

"Lucy, fix me something to eat."

She looked around and found Tad's box of potatoes and fried up a skillet full. Tad was getting mighty hungry too and asked if he could have some. Guess Boss wanted to keep them all alive, so he made Lucy fry up some more potatoes for her and Tad. Tad thought he never tasted better taters. Don't think she did either because she sure lost her manners scarfin' her share down.

When darkness fell on the cabin, they all went down for the night. The only difference from the night before, was Tad didn't disturb Boss's rest, so he didn't give Tad a headache.

Chapter Five

*T*he next morning the wind had stopped howling and Boss was tired of the menu.

"Tad, shovel a path to the smokehouse," he ordered, "and then to the shed."

Boss even allowed Tad to feed his dogs saying that we might need them later.

Though Tad hiked up and down the mountain to town, he wondered if Boss rode a horse and if he did, where was it? And where was Jim's horse? He looked around outside and when he didn't see any sign of a horse figured they were either buried in the snow or went back to town on their own. In an emergency, the dogs could pull the sled, but they were getting old and not as strong as they used to be. Tad was fond of them thus he kind of pampered them.

They went back inside, and Boss even let Tad sit in his favorite chair. Then he was surprised to hear Boss tell Lucy that he felt like a little stroll with her would be good.

Now Tad thought Boss had lost his mind. Nobody in their right mind would go tramping around in all that snow. But he made Lucy bundle up and pulled her out the door. In spite of himself, he felt a little sorry for that troublesome woman. He just hoped Boss wouldn't part with her like he did Jim. Of course, what he really wanted was for Boss to disappear.

But he didn't disappear and brought Lucy back in what seemed a short time. Boss was mad! They came in stamping and shaking snow. She was just really shaking and went over to the fireplace where she fell down on her knees to get warm.

As if Boss wasn't able, he made her get up and put more logs on the fire. Tad was glad because he'd been getting chilly waiting for them. Although Boss had tied his chair to the stove, he was afraid to move because if he turned that stove over, he could burn the cabin down. Besides, he cut those trees down, trimmed every log and built this nice cabin from the ground up. And he didn't want it burned down.

After Boss had set by the fireplace long enough to get warm, he told Tad the next morning, he was going with both of them for another walk.

Good, he thought as he was getting cabin fever. He just hoped he didn't get a fever from getting cold outside but with his luck lately, that could be the outcome of the next day's outing.

That night Tad thought they must've been bad because they went to bed without any supper. Well, him and Lucy anyway. Boss was chewing on something and Tad wished it would've choked him.

Plus, Boss drunk the last drop of his whiskey, didn't

save any for medical emergencies. There weren't any doctors out here either, just dumb city slickers. How stupid can you get?

Boss was really getting on his nerves. He began wondering if it wouldn't be better to be shot to death than to starve to death. Still he didn't trust Boss to kill him, probably just wound him and then he'd bleed to death real slow and painful.

He shut his eyes, because if looks could kill he'd stare a hole straight through Boss's ugly head.

The next morning Lucy did make some biscuits and fried up more potatoes. She found a hunk of cheese Tad was saving for a special occasion, and he figured this must be that special occasion because it did taste really good. They were going to need their energy because Boss wanted all of them to go for a walk.

There was still all that snow to get through but against Tad's better judgment, he said, "Boss I might be able to rig us up some snowshoes." They actually only needed one pair because he had two pairs in the shed. When Boss asked about the dogs and the sled, Tad told him they'd better be kept for an emergency because they didn't have too many trips to town in them. Guess he believed him because he let him make Lucy a pair of shoes out of an old barrel and they set off. To where, Tad had no idea.

Boss made Tad lead and he could only hope Boss didn't make a false step, fall down and shoot him in the back. He was told to uncover the path down to town and said, "Ok, I'll try to find it, but it is a little buried."

How was he supposed to find the trail in three feet of snow? Only someone not used to the mountains would say something that dumb.

After traveling a while, Boss made them stop, grabbed Lucy by the collar and said, "Ok, now, I'm getting real tired of this, where in this God forsaken mountain is it?"

What's the 'It' they keep talking about, Tad wondered. He was getting more than a little tired too, and the cold didn't cool the temper rising in him. He didn't take lightly to a woman being abused. How disgusting! But, what could he do to get rid of this trash, Boss? He started thinking and looking. There had to be a way out of this. Boss was in 'HIS' territory, so he started looking for something as a weapon.

In the meantime, Lucy started crying again and Tad sure was starting to hate that sound. What he wanted to hear was the approach of a posse. Even an old bear or cougar, anything, to distract Boss so he could pick up a branch and knock some sense into him. He wanted to be "Boss".

Then he heard Lucy say,

"I don't know where 'It' is, with all the snow I can't see anything. I put it under a big pile of rocks near a big tree just a short time before we got to Tad's. Jim didn't know either, so you killed him for nothing. I'm trying Boss, please don't hurt me!"

About then, Tad exploded, "I don't know what 'It' is that you're lookin' for, but I do know this snow ain't going away until spring and that won't be for another month. You two are drivin' me crazy!"

He turned his back to them expectin' to feel pain from a bullet in the back, but he didn't. Instead Boss said,

"You know, if I didn't need you, you'd be dead right now. And frankly, I'm tempted to shoot you anyways, but I need you to do one more thing. And you, little witch," he said looking at Lucy, "have got about twenty-four more hours to live, unless you start remembering where it is! Let's get back to the cabin. I'm freezin' out here."

Chapter Six

*T*hey had a good supper that night, venison from the smoke house, canned corn and crunchy biscuits. Tad and Lucy were allowed to eat first before ole' Boss did. He ate the leftovers after he tied them up. The good thing for Lucy was they had found more rope in the shed, so she didn't have to do her vanishing act into the trunk. When she could, she hid the rope in her clothes. Tad wondered if Boss was losing his appetite, letting them go first and then he noticed him kind of picking at his food. He seemed to be thinking or pondering about something, maybe he was just getting plain tired.

Considering all this, Tad's hopes rose. He didn't know if it was the venison, corn or biscuits but he came up with an idea. He remembered a big twisted tree where he always set a trap that had a lot of dead limbs lying around its base. It seemed the wild creatures liked that tree too. It kind of reminded him of life with its many twists and turns. And good too, just close enough to the path that Boss wouldn't get suspicious when he led him there. His next prayer was that the trap which would still be set. He had bigger game to catch, or at least startle.

"Boss," he said, "I think I can lead you to that big tree where Lucy left 'It'."

Boss replied, "Ok, tomorrow morning, and you better be ready."

Tad still didn't know what 'It' was, but he figured he could play a trick on ole' Boss and get the gun away from him.

It was kind of hard to get to sleep because his mind kept playing that 'freedom tape'. But it must have finally shut down because the next thing he knew Boss was shoving that pistol in his back telling him to get up.

Ole' cry baby was banging around the stove and the coffee was smelling real good! He needed a cup, real strong and black. Another special occasion that morning, she had found the ingredients for pancakes. We need something to stick to our ribs on freedom trail, but Ma always said it was the oatmeal that stuck to your ribs. Of course, it could have been because it was cheaper too.

She had quit sniffling and boss sat quiet at the table watching her. Now, Tad was the quiet thinking type so naturally he liked it when everything was quiet. The only motion was when Boss started clothing up for outside, and he told Lucy and Tad to do the same. When they went out Boss didn't stop and let him take care of his dogs, but he figured if his plan worked, he could do it later. The dogs weren't getting any exercise so they shouldn't be very hungry. Unlike people, dogs don't eat when they are bored.

They trudged downward away from the cabin struggling through the snow. It took about half a day to get to the tree where Tad was leading Boss. They were about four feet from the tree when Tad stopped and said,

"I need a break to take a leak."

He went in a circle to get behind the tree for his privacy and as he hoped, Boss didn't follow him. Instead, Boss stepped forward and snap went the trap. He didn't know if it actually caught him, but it did catch him off guard. And when Boss fell backwards, Tad shot around that tree like a bolt of lightning to strike him.

Lucy picked up the gun that fell from Boss's cold hand so Boss couldn't shoot him. Tad straddled him using his hands like the blade of a guillotine. WHAM, he chopped him. He didn't need any tree branch. It felt good to get rid of that frustration. BAM, BAM, he struck Boss two more times! Tad was not only frustrated but mad as a hornet. Then he heard Lucy yelling something that didn't make any sense.

"Stop, Tad, stop or I'll shoot!" she hollered again. Good grief, she had picked up Boss's gun and was aiming it at him.

Now doggone it, he wasn't the enemy, Boss was. Still, as he had already learned, he couldn't trust her either. So, he stopped pounding on Boss and stood up.

"What do you think you're doing, girl?", Tad said.

He just saved her life and now she was threating his.

"Get your wits together, we're in this together. Give me that pistol!", he said.

"No!" she screamed, "I don't trust you!"

Tad tried to stay calm,

"You may not trust me, but you need me. And if I was you, I'd be a little bit worried about what ole' Boss is gonna do to me and you, when he comes around. So, you better give me that rope you hid so I can tie him up.", Tad insisted.

She hesitated, stared at Boss and then at Tad.

"Well, I guess you know this mountain better than him. But how do I know you won't run out on me like you did before when we were married?" she added.

Tad kind of chuckled, it was the first amusing thing anyone had said all day.

"It" might be worth a little more now.

She dropped her hand holding the gun but didn't turn the gun over to Tad. She told him to tie the varmint up.

Tad told her they had two choices. We can keep going towards town without any supplies, or go back and get some, and then start out in the morning. His sense of humor, or maybe of right and wrong, created in him the image of ole Boss sitting in that chair all night. Fortunately for ole' Boss, he was too big for the trunk. Lucy broke into his thoughts.

"Isn't too hard to figure that one out, is it?" She said. "It's not too hard to figure out who's keeping the gun either."

They struggled back to the cabin, half carrying ole' Boss. Tad was sure tempted to just drop him and let him fend for himself. Then his conscience had to be heard. "You can't do that man, you're no killer! Even if you think he deserves it," Tad said to himself. Ok, he'd let the sheriff decide Boss's punishment, or God.

That brought a relief to Tad's mind and Boss even began to feel lighter. They made it back to the cabin and Tad made supper. Ironically, the one with the power and also the cook, became the 'Boss.' Tad decided on the food; venison and corn again and maybe another good idea. He made biscuits too, not wanting to leave out any ingredient for good ideas.

And guess what, it worked! Very sweetly, he asked the new Boss to step outside with him for a few minutes. She stepped out, too, and going to the shed he managed to stumble into her which threw her off balance. He wrestled her to the ground and was blessed again, the gun slipped from her fingers.

Yes, he thought, I got it, and then she started that awful whimpering again.

"Please, don't shoot, I'll be good to you.", she said.

Well Tad was Boss now and he was going to get some answers. He stood tall over her kneeling at his feet. (Day of Judgement.) Using his first Boss tone, he said,

"You got one chance to tell me what this is all about. And I mean right now."

He hoped his words sounded mean enough for her to see flame in his eyes. It worked too because she started telling him her story;

"There was a rich old widower who came into the saloon where I worked about every night and said it made him feel good. Not only the booze, but he loved the music and dancing, and also seemed to like my company. In fact, so much so, that one night he gave me this beautiful sapphire neckless, which I never took off."

"So did Peter, that's Boss's real name. His companions were Thomas and Mitchell. They also liked the fun in the bar and liked my company. After making my acquaintance, they asked about the old man, Mr. Bigelow."

She continued, "They'd already heard he was a big man in the town. He had made a lot of money in mining, and actually had helped build the town. The railroad just being there helped too. He lived in the biggest house at the edge of the main street by himself. He did have a housekeeper (of sorts) who was young and pretty. Her name was Madeline and she was a looker but not a hooker. But she, unlike me, managed to hold onto a husband whom she was able to spend the nights with and had Sundays off for church attending."

"It all seemed to be working until one Monday morning when Madeline went to work and was surprised to find the back door unlocked. But not seeing anything wrong, she went into the kitchen and made coffee for her boss.

She took it into the library as usual and at first glance Mr. Bigelow wasn't there. She walked over to the desk and much to her dismay, found the poor old guy lying behind it. On a closer look, it appeared he was dead."

"Madeline screamed and ran from the room and through the house. Using the front door, for the first time, she ran out onto the front porch, down the steps, and across the yard to the street. She kept screaming and running like a mad woman down into town where she finally collapsed on the sidewalk in front of the bank."

"People started gathering around her. Some probably thought the bank had refused her credit or maybe was taking back her little cottage. This was happening a lot since the railroad quit running through town. Finally, she managed to gasp out,

"The sheriff, get the sheriff!"

She continued her story, "One man named Joe, broke out of the circle surrounding her and ran to the sheriff's office just a few buildings away. He busted in through the door to find the sheriff dozing in his chair. Startled, the sheriff jumped up ripping his gun from its holster and lucky for Joe he recognized him and didn't shoot."

The sheriff said, "What's wrong with you Joe? Why did you come charging in here like a run-away bull?"

"Joe told him something was happening at the bank and the sheriff thought he meant somebody was robbing it so he grabbed his shotgun, throwing it at Joe since the town couldn't afford a deputy figuring Joe would have to do. He ran out the door with Joe right behind him trying to tell him he was getting overly excited as nothing much happened in their little town. Joe was just a cowboy and the only thing he ever chased were cows."

"So, Joe and the sheriff ran down the sidewalk,

broke through the crowd and ran right past the fallen girl into the bank."

"Later Joe laughed as he said, 'What a sight, me and the sheriff charging into the bank waving our guns. The teller, who was kind of deaf, hadn't heard the young girl screaming when she fell in front of the bank. Still, he should've seen the bunch of people through the bank's big window. Maybe he was bored, he didn't know, or half asleep, but he woke up real soon and was startled to see me and the sheriff waving our guns around.'"

"What's going on?" the teller asked the sheriff.

"The sheriff was also plenty surprised because it was evident there wasn't any crime in progress; unless sleeping on the job was a crime, then that being the case the sheriff and most of the business proprietors, except the ever busy saloon, were guilty as charged," Lucy laughed then proceeded on with her story.

"The sheriff turned to his instant deputy and demanded an explanation. Unfortunately, he was just as confused as the sheriff. He told him how the girl was lying on her back screaming for help and calling for someone to get the sheriff."

"I thought something was happening in the bank guess you better go talk to her."

"Irritated, the sheriff turned and stomped outside to find the girl in question. She was now able to sit up and speak so the sheriff leaned over and asked her what was wrong."

Shaking, Madeline said, "Mr. Bigelow is dead."

"Evidently that didn't surprise the sheriff because

he told the girl the man was old and had almost outlived the town so what was the big deal?"

The sheriff said, "Get a hold of yourself girl, because no one lives forever, and your boss was no exception."

"But you don't understand," she cried out. "He's been shot!"

Chapter Seven

*O*f course, in their little town, murder hardly ever happened. So, Lucy explained how nervous the people started to get, especially when a woman threw her arms in the air and started crying out to the Lord, "Save us Lord, come quickly Lord Jesus. Save us from this awful generation of ungodliness."

Lucy went on, "The others began murmuring among themselves. Some started feeling a little edgy, wondering how or when the killer came there, or was it someone living there with hard feelings for Mr. Bigelow? And then another man spoke out saying anyone who managed to become that wealthy must've made an enemy or two along the way.

Next the sheriff helped Madeline stand up and started walking her back down the street with his new deputy and most of the concerned citizens following them.

At this point Tad asked Lucy, "And where were you at this point?"

Lucy answered, "Quite a way down the road with my new friend, Jack, the trucker. But bad news has a fast way of traveling and when we reached his first town the people there had already heard about the murder. The telephone and telegraph were good inventions, but I wasn't to be outdone, I immediately found a car with the key in the ignition and borrowed it to drive myself on down the road. I went through a few towns before ending up here."

"That story don't make any sense at all." Tad said. "Why'd you run away from there? Did you have something to do with the old man's death?" Tad was still trying to make sense of her story that didn't make any sense.

"No!" She said, "I didn't kill Mr. Bigelow but I saw who did."

"What! What do you mean you saw it?" Tad asked, still not believing he was getting an honest answer from Lucy.

"Well," she said, "I told you about Pete asking me a bunch of questions about Mr. Bigelow. Then one night he and his two partners came in the bar and kinda huddled together at a table back in the corner. Didn't pay any attention to me, just kept whispering among themselves."

"A short time passed, and they got up, left some money on the table for their beers then went out the side door into the alley. I don't know how, but I just knew they were up to something. I was kinda bored and feeling a bit heroic I put my coat on and with my hood up I slipped out after them."

"They went down the dark alley to the street that

surrounded the town. I just knew they were up to no good. Otherwise, why would they be sneaking around the back ways? At the end of town, I saw them go up through Mr. Bigelow's yard and start looking through his windows. Then the next thing I knew, they'd managed to open up one and were crawling through it. I snuck up behind them and then on towards the window where a light showed through."

"Old Mr. Bigelow was at his desk and behind him was what looked like a hole in the wall, with a door on it."

"For Heaven's sake, I remember thinking, he has a safe in the wall!"

"I remember how proud he was of that picture that used to hang there. He showed it to me one night when I helped him home. Too much music and drinking for him and he was shaky on his legs. He told me that picture was painted by a famous painter."

"The painter was 'Vam Go', or something like that, he told me. He said he bought it for his wife on her fiftieth birthday. He said she loved it and he didn't know she was an art lover. He kind of hinted about how he could've bought her a herd of cattle for what that one picture cost. His wife had laughed and said she'd rather have the picture."

"Yes sir, that little lady had class, married me didn't she, Mr. Bigelow boasted."

"I remember laughing, thinking I'd have chosen the cattle, said Lucy."

"Well," Lucy continued. "The next thing I saw

was the door opening into the room and those three sneaky crooks stood there holding guns. Then poor Mr. Bigelow made the worst mistake of his life when he tried to take a gun from his desk drawer."

"He had brought his gun into the bar one day to show me and told how he kept it in that desk in the library room in case he ever needed it. I'm sorry because it was so big and different looking. I later told Peter about it thinking he'd get a kick out of hearing about it. It looked bigger than the old man's arm." Then she stopped talking.

Tad said, "Go on Lucy, what happened?"

Lucy continued, "Thomas knocked Mr. Bigelow out of his chair and then Peter went up to the desk where a stack of bills was laid. He grabbed them and turned around to the wall. He stuck his hand into the hole and pulled out more bills, then again, but this time he had a hand full of jewelry. He pulled a sack out of his back pocket and started stuffing it. Man, that hidey hole had a lot of stuff in it. He filled up his bag really big."

"When he was through at the safe, Peter moved sideways and looked down at the old man, then just like he was swatting a fly, he shot him! They started running out the room and I ran over to a clump of bushes to hide. I saw them climb out of the window and head back the way they came. But they veered off and went into the woods. I didn't know what to do, I wanted to follow them, but I was scared. Then that scent of treasure called to me and I followed it. It wasn't long till I caught up to where the three of them had stopped and were arguing about what to do with the money. Peter seemed to win out."

He said, "Look, we can't chance carryin' this bag into town to get our car. Let's bury it here. Then we'll come back with our car and some grub and high-tail it outta town."

"The others agreed and started walking back, they almost caught me, but I managed to hide. Then what I saw made me want to die, well not die but I didn't want to see what I did see."

She shut her mouth and eyes, bowed her head, and shuddered.

"What?" Tad asked, "What did you see?"

After a few minutes she went on.

"I saw Peter reach down into his boot and pull out a knife. He stabbed Thomas in the back and before Mitchell saw what he was doing, Peter stabbed him too. Then Peter wiped the knife off in the grass, stuck it back in his boot and walked off towards town."

"After he was gone, I snuck over to where they stashed the loot, moved the branches and trash covering it and took the bag. Unfortunately for me, I snagged my necklace on a branch leaving it to dangle in plain sight. I didn't worry about losing it because what was in the bag could have bought me a thousand new necklaces."

"I ran back towards town but by a different way than Peter had gone. I knew a truck stop was at the edge of town and I found a trucker by the name of Jack ready to leave, so I went with him."

Tad couldn't help wondering if what she told him

was to get him to take her away like the trucker. But he didn't ask because he couldn't believe anything she said. He wouldn't set much stock in her storytelling about that night if he hadn't met her buddy Peter. So now what was he to do? He knew he was sick of them both. But being a sensible man, he knew the best thing was to get them to town and let the law deal with them.

Of course, Lucy had to come up with an alternate plan. She said that she would only go along with Tad's plan, if he let her keep half the money and promise not to tell about how she had hidden the money and stuff.

Lucy added that since the old widower didn't have any family and her being his closest and best friend, she knew he'd want her to have his money.

Tad thought there'd probably be a reward for that killer Peter, and he could have it all himself. Plus, then this was the kicker, she would share half of her inheritance with him when they found it after the snow melted. It'd mean a new life for her and it sure would make Tad's life a lot easier too. It made sense in a kind of odd way, so he agreed with her plan but later thought, "What did I get myself into this time?"

Chapter Eight

*T*he next morning, though he hated to do it, he hooked up his dogs, got supplies ready and put them and Lucy on the sled. Oh yeah, he hooked Peter to the sled too, figuring he was good for something. He could help the dogs pull Lucy back to town. He didn't take to the idea until Tad got his whip out and snapped it over Peter's head a few times. The trusting ole' dogs thought it meant for them to get started and poor ole' Pete had to hurry or get run over.

But the good thing was, he didn't have to swing that whip again. Tad thought this would probably be the last trip to town for his old friends, the dogs, and he prayed that after a month of resting they'd manage to get back home where they would truly retire. It took two days, but they all made it.

He thought he'd be glad to see civilization again, but that was before he found himself in such company.

He went to the jail house where he and Lucy told the sheriff their agreed-upon story. Peter was wanted for questioning and Lucy nailed him to the gallows. Also, there was a reward. Unfortunately, now he was stuck with his loving spouse. Good fortune and bad fortune found him that day. They went looking for Jim to tell him the good news but couldn't find him.

They knew Boss wasn't lying when he told them what he'd done to Jim. Still, they hung on to a slim hope of finding him alive. They asked the sheriff if he'd heard anything about Jim, and he said Jim was seen riding out with Peter a while back but that was the last time anybody had seen him. What really concerned the sheriff was when the two horses they'd ridden out on returned to the stables without anyone riding them. Also, supplies, bed rolls and two rifles were still on the horses.

It now seemed likely, that they'd be searching for Jim, or what was left of him, come spring. Tad was feeling pretty lonely and that was something new for him. But good friends are hard to find.

He didn't find anything else to keep them in town so they loaded up a few luxuries like real toilet paper, bars of store-bought soap, butter, couple of those Havana cigars and so that Miss Lucy could feel good, he got her some perfume so she would smell good too. He couldn't help wondering why someone didn't make animal perfume so they could smell good! But spoiling herself didn't improve his sweet-smelling partner's attitude. She didn't want to leave town till spring. He put his foot down to that and said, "No way."

He then informed her she'd better follow their agreement to lay low until spring and they sure couldn't do that with a lot of bored, snoopy town folks, around, so they lit out. Going back to the cabin through the snow would remind her of how she needed him, then and later. He was determined to get her holed up, so he didn't have to hang around constantly. He could go about his business of hunting, trapping and exploring.

"Wouldn't it be something, like an act of a giving God if I could discover her ill-gotten treasure? That sure would make a better believer out of me," he thought, but it didn't happen."

The weeks crawled by, the weather got a little warmer each day and the snow began to melt. He was praying for an early spring. He had cabin fever and being around a complaining woman didn't help. Also, as the snow reached a lower level, he figured it would be dangerous to stray too far from her because she might just try to slip out and run away!

Finally, he decided it was time to start searching, along with her, so they spent days outside looking. It was still cold, so it limited their time but then one fine day they found 'It'!

Oh, what a time of celebration and right away they headed into town. It was great! Because if you truly want to celebrate in a proper style you gotta be in a proper place. On the mountains was not it! But civilization with its lights, music and liquid refreshments was. There were some pretty good cooks there too, and he was really hungry for a good meal not a home-cooked one.

When they reached town, they got a room in the hotel, first class, no boarding house for them. They got cleaned up and went out on the town, it was great. After a couple hours and a couple drinks, ok more than a couple drinks, he decided to take the Missus, who had started looking better, back to get some rest and shut eye. But in their night of celebration Tad forgot that she may have been looking better but she was still the same sneaky conniving bar girl inside. That was evident when he woke up alone in the hotel room. Broke!

He couldn't tell you how he felt, other than a bit hung over. He was mad as a bull at himself, about as much as he was at her. Still there was an upside, he didn't have to put up with her anymore. Hurray for sanity! And he was sure smarter from the experience. It'd be a cold day you know, where before he'd trust any woman like he'd had his ma and grandma.

Yep, times were changing and so was he, he was really thankful to the good Lord for what he did with the reward money he received. He invested in land, a ranch. You see he didn't want to live on the beach, and he was getting to feel that up there in the mountains could be a kind of dangerous place, look what all that'd happened to him the last few months. Besides his Pa would finally be proud of him because he always had to work for someone else and he sure hated it. He wanted to be Boss. So now he owned his own spread. He would be working for himself.

Also, fortunately, he had met a young couple of city slickers, new in town, looking for a secluded get-away from all the hustle and bustle of city life. His cabin was just what they were looking for and when they learned about his dogs, they knew it was just what they wanted. Being dog lovers, they promised Tad they would take good care of his old dogs. He gladly sold it to them and said good-bye to his old friends.

Since the landowner's wife wanted to go back East, all that was left to take possession of the ranch was to move in. She was a city girl and probably so was her husband because they sold him the place for about a third of what it was worth. When they signed the agreement and he got the money, they said it'd only take them a week to get packed up and out. Then added, "There are a few cowhands, real good men, who work the ranch and handled the cattle. They will probably stay on."

Tad thought, "Being as I'm new at the job I'll appreciate any help I can get and I'm looking forward to ranch life."

Still he couldn't help thinking, a little bit's nice but a little bit more would be better. He was thinking about that bag. She sure didn't need it all! Besides she put one over on him and it smarted. His EGO hurt.

"Bet I could find that treasure again," he thought.

So, the big debate started that day, him against himself, greed against greed, and good decisions against bad decisions. He wrestled with the giant all day and night and by the next morning he'd made up his mind. He loaded up his old pickup truck that he kept in town and headed out to find the girl and her treasure sack. This time he knew what 'It' was he was looking for.

Funny though how things turn out, the treasure Tad found wasn't what he was looking for.....

Dedicated to my granddaughter
Caitlyn or Katie:

Katie

Also; Dedicated to my brothers Billy and Bob:

Billy   *Bob*

'A New Call'

Chapter One

Riding the rails

*T*he lonesome sound of a train awakened the man as he was being hauled along across the miles to California where his uncle had moved to and where he had first traveled the rails.

This time Bob's going and his choice of riding the rails were for completely different reasons than when he first went. The irony of it brought a twisted grimace to his thin lips hidden in a mass of grey whiskers. How many times as a youth had he heard this same music call out to him, 'come, come ride me,' and it seemed to sooth his troubled heart. As a youth the thought of freedom and escape from his miserable life was all he thought about. He'd heard about the gold found in California and thought that gold would be the answer to all of his problems. Someday, he had promised his self, someday.

That someday came a few years later when he had just turned thirteen. With a small purse and big dreams, he picked up his satchel and snuck aboard a train. The box car was as dark as the air around him. But he was not afraid, well maybe a little bit, yet his excitement overrode his fear. He snuggled back into a corner behind a stack of boxes. The rhythm of the tracks swaddled him like his mother's womb and in spite of his cramped position.

He fell asleep until he felt something on his shoulder and with a start, he scrambled up crying out;

"Get away, get away." He had visions of some big animal clawing at his shoulder.

"Oh Lord," he shouted. "Help me."

"Hush, hush up kid before you get us all caught," a strange voice whispered.

He looked around in a frenzy. Thankfully, he realized it wasn't a wild animal, just a vagrant. He could barely make him out in the dim early morning light sneaking through the box car slats. Then he saw the outline of this man who was down on his knees. Somehow, that prayerful position gave him the courage to say,

"Please sir, don't hurt me. I'm sorry."

"For what, kid? I'm the one who scared you!" replied the man.

Well, that was forty years ago and now he was the old man greeting a young runaway out on what probably was his first trip on a train. The last time the train was stopped, he saw the boy climb aboard. Therefore, thinking it was up to him to make things right he held out his hand saying,

"Hi young man, I'm Bob, what's your name?"

"I'm Billy," but before he could take his hand another traveler, not so friendly, interrupted and smirked, saying, "Well, I'm Sir, and I really don't care who you are but I do care about all the confounded noise you're making. So, keep quiet!"

"Oh," the young man thought. "Guess he ain't had that first cup of coffee yet. Hope he gets one soon."

Then Billy laughed softly thinking he wouldn't be getting one soon unless they stowed away a cooking stove among all these boxes. Plenty of wood from them for a fire though. Then he snickered again.

Sir grabbed him by both shoulders this time and pulled him face to face where Billy then saw the threat in his eyes as he said;

"Not another sound out of you, do you hear me?" "Yes Sir," replied Billy.

What seemed hours later, but actually was only a couple of minutes, Sir then said in a low voice;

"You don't want to wake the others which you already would've if they hadn't swigged that moonshine last night. When they do wake up, I don't think they're going to be in a good mood. So be still!"

Then Bob interrupted Sir and said, "Calm down and let me think about this situation."

After what seemed a lot of time Billy thought,

"Guess he's getting old because it's taking him a mighty long time to think, or maybe like old folks do, he'd nodded off."

Billy nodded off too then hours later he felt a change that woke him up and realized the train seemed to be slowing down. Uncertainty caused him to nudge Bob.

"Sorry, but what's happening," he asked?

Bob stirred, looked up and the sun found a crack in the door that showed Billy his face clearly. "He looked like he'd ridden a lot of tracks since he was so old," he surmised.

Bob said, "Well kid, I guess you have two choices because we'll be pulling into the next stop in about ten minutes."

Billy wondered how he knew this unless he'd traveled this way before. But he didn't say anything. Respect your elders was one of the things his mother taught him.

Then Bob said, "I don't know if any of this stuff, pointing around at the boxes, will be getting unloaded here or not. Also, I don't know if any of those troublesome inspectors or detectives, or whatever they are, will be checking out this car. So, either get ready to jump off or hide deep as you can and see what happens. The worst thing would be if they catch you and take you to jail."

He laughed, "Or maybe they'd just send you back home. If you do jump, hopefully you won't break a leg or something. It's up to you kid, but I'm hiding, I'm too old to jump."

So, Billy started thinking. "He knew he could jump and wasn't afraid of breaking anything unless they were going over a bridge. If he hit the bridge that would smart or if he fell in the water he might drown, he couldn't swim."

That thought, made staying on the train his best shot. Also, he realized with all his drunken or hungover box car buddies, he was likely to be spotted and caught first.

He'd always hated that he was kind of little, smaller than other boys his age. In fact, other boys picked on him the most, unless you counted the girls who he could relate to when others called him, "Sissy". But maybe this time his size could work to his advantage.

He looked around and decided the nearest corner space looked pretty good. He shifted some boxes to create a hole and crawled through and then reached out and moved a big box in front of his hiding place. Now he thought, "If I can keep from wetting my pants, I'll be ok."

He finished his hiding place just in time before the train stopped. He expected the door to slide open any second, but he waited and waited, and nothing happened.

Then suddenly he felt a jerk, then another, and another. Then he heard a sound. Someone was tooting a horn. Wow, they were moving. Yeah! He moved the box that was his door and crawled out. The old man was just sitting where he'd left him.

Perplexed, Billy asked him, "Why didn't you hide?" His new friend laughed and said, "I put one over on you, didn't I?"

"What! What do you mean?" Billy asked. Then he heard a burst of laughter from Sir and things being moved. Some grumbling was also heard as another man came over to squat before him. He was a ragged, dirty, and unshaven man about his stepdad's age of forty. Not a very encouraging sight. He was kind of shaking and all he could say was, "Ooh."

Then, that made them laugh even harder but still it was a good sign, he thought. "Maybe they won't kill me, or hurt me too bad, just take my money, the little bit of clothing I brought and take my pocketknife. He didn't think they'd want his small Bible. Probably couldn't read or if they could, wouldn't want to think or remember much about sin. Because if they believed in God, why were they in that hard situation, or was this their idea of Hades on wheels?"

Then the old man who had taken him in, as a sidekick lashed out at the others, "Ok, ok, that's enough out of you guys. Shut up, he's just a kid and if he hasn't already wet his pants, he probably needs to take a leak. I know I sure do, so get out of the way."

Billy surmised they must have some kind of respect for Bob, as they started shifting around to let him through to the door. Billy followed the old man feeling a bit safer. Also, he felt a lot fuller, but how, where, could he empty out?

The old man reached the door and after some huffing and puffing, slid it open about a foot.

"Young'uns first," he said and stepped aside. But Billy just stood there not certain what to do.

"Confound it, kid, take it out and let it go. Just aim it out the door, ok? If you have to do the number two, there's an old bucket over there in the corner," he said, pointing toward the back.

Lucky for him, he hadn't eaten the day before, so he

didn't need the bucket. He stepped aside after watering the landscape and made his way back to his corner. After the rest of them took their turn at the door, he saw one of them head for the bucket in the corner. He shut his eyes because he didn't want to see any bare bottoms, but he couldn't help hearing the small explosions and then a yelp.

"Where is that catalog?"

The others laughed and then one moved a crate he was sitting on, reached under it and brought out, of all things, a beat-up Sears catalog. He tossed it over into the corner where it must have landed on the recipient's head as he yelped again,

"Oh, you bum, think you're smart, do you? Well tomorrow's another day. Yeah."

Chapter Two

*T*hings seem to settle down after the commotion. Then one of them produced a flask of something and passed it around. When it got to the kid, he wiped the mouth of it off, took a long drink. Spitting it out, he ran toward the open door, coughing and gagging. He thought he'd be drinking water and though he'd never drunk liquor, he found the taste to be nastier than anything he'd ever put in his mouth.

Again, the jovial sounds bounced off the wall. It wasn't pleasant to Billy and as in other times, when he was laughed at, he put his hands over his ears. He had such a sad and dejected look on his face the old man took pity on him, punched his shoulder and said;

"Hey, guess I better set you straight on a few things."

He paused waiting for the young man's reaction. Billy took a long searching look into the old one's eyes and thought, "Guess Bob wanted him to know he had some control over the situation."

"Well young'un, this life on the road can get pretty boring sometimes and when a chance comes to have a little fun, you just grab a hold of it and do whatever comes to your mind. I can see you're going to have to get a sense of humor about you. You've chosen a hard ride and if laughing helps you hold on you better learn that quickly."

Then he paused to see if anything was sinking in. Billy kind of squirmed around and hung his head like he was letting it sink in.

Then Bob said, "Another thing, maybe more important, don't believe everything you hear or see because life's a lie. Most people you get to know are liars and actors using life's scenes as stages to get what they want or think they want. And they don't always get what they need, or even more important, what they deserve. Unless of course, you believe that book I saw you pull out last night."

"Yeah, I've also read it," Bob nodded. "And it talks about a day of judgment, so guess everyone eventually does get what he or she deserves. I've met a lot of girls worse than any man I ever knew."

Then the old man stopped talking. With his eyes focused on something, seemingly far away, maybe thinking about what he'd said too. Then the young man spoke up;

"Well thanks, you're a great teacher, or maybe better yet, a great preacher. What I really need to know, is how long till we come to another stop?"

"So much for words of wisdom," thought Bob. He shook his head and grinned. Then he said; "The next stop will be when this train picks up new passengers."

"And obviously, since we know that last stop wasn't

Memphis but just a place to stop for new passengers, we should hit Memphis about sundown."

"Oh man," the kid cried. "I'll be dead by then."

"What?" The old man asked. "I ain't had a drop of water since yesterday," the boy explained.

"Well, aren't you the lucky one," Bob said. "Hey Slim, bring that jug over here."

Then a real skinny hand came out from the darkness of the back wall opposite the door. It was holding a moonshine jug.

"No," cried the boy recognizing it from those like he saw his dad swig from, the nasty evil stuff that changed him into a devil!

"You're a piece of work, Billy," shouted Bob. "But then again, maybe you're learning to be a bit more careful."

"It's water, but don't get your hopes up. It sure isn't crystal clean. It's kind of muddy, beings as it's from the river. Still it'll wet your whistle for now."

As if signaled, the hand turned into a long skinny arm, then into a still longer body and Billy could see why he was called Slim. As well as a skinny body, the man had a long skinny head and Billy watched as he emerged from behind a stack of boxes out into the open center of the railroad car. It looked like his life had been one of slim pickin's. He felt kind of sorry for him, so he met him halfway. Or maybe he was just plain dying for a drink of water, muddy or not! He grabbed the jug, and then sensibly took a short sip, testing the waters, as they say. Actually, it was water and probably the best he ever tasted. In fact, as a bit dribbled down the side it looked like chocolate milk which he loved.

"Don't reckon you're hungry, are you, young'un?" asked Bob.

"Yes, I sure am," replied Billy.

The old man shouted out, "Any of you got a bite of food to spare? All I got to chew on is tobacco."

There was silence, then a mumbling from someone with a mouthful of something and then he spoke more clearly.

Slim said, "Reckon I can spare a piece of this jerky. Here kid, come and get it. I ain't servin' it up. But hurry up, for I change my mind."

Billy scrambled over and took it out of his hand, "Thanks Sir, I don't know your name."

"Well I like being called sir, but you know my name is 'Slim', and pointing to a guy sitting on the floor by him. He's 'Simple', as his actions will show ya. And that hairy guy over there is Sir."

Billy looked at the meat and thought, "hope he ain't already chewed on it." He immediately felt ashamed.

"Don't look a gift horse in the mouth," was a favorite of his mom's whenever she got a handout at the church or that welfare place, which made you stand in line for hours. In fact, Billy felt somehow it wasn't free or a gift because it took forever to wait for it. He thought they earned it. "Be patient, all in good time, or God's time," was another of her sayings, also sometimes the preacher's or someone else declared, "Hallelujah!"

This made the youngster realize he was starting

to miss her and home and wondered, "Is she missing me or relieved she doesn't have to look out for me?" He knew his dad would be glad he'd gone. He always said he wasn't good for anything and wasn't worth a plug nickel. Whatever kind of coin that was? Well he'd show him! He was on his way west, to the gold fields of California, and not for coins but for gold nuggets.

He could hardly wait, but again reflected on his mother's advice about patience. He had to be patient. She was so wise. Yet, he shook his head, wondering, how could someone as smart as her and knowing so much, hook up with someone as dumb as his dad, and then later, his stepdad?

It must have been some kind of charity on her part, only to end up living on charity like she does. Grownups, who could understand them? But he'd noted they did get dumber as they got older. Hope I don't live that long. Still, some of them looked pretty happy, like the lady in the apartment next door. She lived alone and nobody ever seemed to call on her. And she'd lost most of her weight, her teeth, and her hair. Oh yeah, her eyesight too, she squinted a lot and she could never remember where she put anything, or even people's names.

Yet she laughed and laughed, and sang, and talked, mostly to herself. But why not, she wasn't suffering doing without, she was happy. And she made other people around her happy too, causing them to laugh, maybe at her, but still laughter's good for the soul, and yes, Mom said that too!

Still Billy never heard a preacher say that or he

hadn't ever read it in the Bible which was supposed to tell you everything you needed to know. Well enough of this thinking, it made him sleepy using his brain this much, more likely his empty stomach was emptying his brain. 'Good night or good day', whatever it was, and the rhythm of the faithful train or God put him to sleep.

Chapter Three

*I*n fact, Billy slept really well as Bob had to wake him up when they actually pulled into Memphis. He told him to grab his things and follow him, then they scrambled out through the door as the train pulled to a stop. Then the other three, Slim, Simple and Sir, popped out right behind them and they all took off running behind the train station.

It only took them a few minutes to reach the main part of town and as Billy looked around, he thought the place looked as poor as where he'd run away from and related to Bob,

"Bob, I hope I didn't just travel in a circle."

"No, no, there's a store with a sign saying Memphis Dry Goods", said Bob.

It had barrels of fruit and vegetables outside that were beautiful. "Hog heaven," Billy thought, drooling. He'd go in and buy something.

But as he was about to go in the old men grabbed stuff out of the boxes and barrels and shoved it into their shirts and pants pockets. Then they grabbed him and pulled him in between their taller bodies and started dragging him down the street. Not a minute too soon as a man in an apron come out the front door of the store and yelled,

"Get your thieving, no account selves out of here before I call the cops!"

They started running faster, if you could call it that, limping and shuffling was more like it. Billy couldn't help much as he was laughing so hard and wondered why they were running from that silly man in an apron. Though he was wearing a lady's apron, he sure didn't sound like a lady with the language he had used.

Then they rounded a corner and went into an alley. By that time, the men were huffing and puffing, and Billy felt he was pulling them along. Luckily, they saw a big metal garbage box and ducked behind it. Billy was laughing so hard he thought his stomach would burst and sadly not from being filled up with food. They all fell over on him, grappling to cover his mouth and hissing like a bunch of snakes.

Finally, when all was still, he could make out their words of "Hush, hush up, right now! Hush up before I choke you," Slim whispered.

The words made him think of when his mother used to rock him asleep with the words, "hush a bye my baby, don't you cry". Only they weren't rocking him to sleep. It felt more like they were pounding him with rock like fists. So that they wouldn't accidentally knock out one of his teeth, he clamped his mouth shut and quit struggling. Seeing that he was under control, they relaxed their hold on him.

When he could breathe, Billy took a deep breath through his nose, "Oh, yuck," he thought. "Wish I hadn't breathed in so deeply". The smell was horrendous. Man, B.O. to the max. They ought to use some of that river water in their jug also to bathe in. Oh, please get away from me." He was practically gagging.

Then God answered his prayer as he felt the others moving away and heard one of them say,

"It looks like we're ok, let's move."

At that point Billy seriously thought about making a break of his own and running away from his cohorts. That stink seemed to illustrate his life. One in which he always seemed to fall back into. He tried to be good and do right, clean his act up, but always ended right back in the mire. Well time for a decision.

Then Bob threw out a lifeline, patting him on the back. What a friend, he wasn't one of them crawling away, he'd stayed at his side. He cared. Billy felt he could trust him, so he asked,

"What'll we do now?"

"We've got a place just up a few blocks, let's go," Bob replied. They crawled out from behind the box and stood up. The others weren't in sight. "Cowards! Well who needs them?", he thought.

The two began walking down the street and Billy was checking everything out. The whole area was pretty bleak. There were lots of big buildings that looked deserted and made the street look kind of sad, like a onetime prosperous place which had fallen into hard times. He wondered what had happened and his imagination went into overtime. No matter the scenario, the reality was it all ended up stark and even in daylight, foreboding. Then unexpectedly, Bob grabbed his arm and took him into one of the buildings. He could tell it was a warehouse of some kind because it had a loading dock. Beside the ramp was a door that appeared to be boarded up but wasn't. Bob slid it open then slipped inside pulling Billy in with him.

It was gloomy inside and Billy knew they were lucky it was daytime because at night it would've been impossible to see three feet ahead. They continued on until what looked like the far side and Bob reached down to the floor and pushed over a stack of lumber revealing a square opening. He sat down on the floor, swung a leg over and down, then swung the other one as the hole started eating him up.

But before his head went out of sight, he told Billy to follow him down the ladder, "Be careful, it's kind of a hard place to land if your feet slip," he cautioned.

Gingerly with some apprehension, the young man followed Bob, climbing down an old iron-rung ladder and being careful, as Bob cautioned. When he reached the bottom, he looked around but could hardly see Bob standing right beside him.

"Now what," he thought because it was hard to see anything, and wouldn't you know it, another nasty smelling odor! This time it wasn't his friends B.O. but moldy smelling, like the hay in an old barn he'd found and played in.

"This way," said Bob and started walking away to

the right. Billy followed, staying close behind and soon they came to a door. When it opened, he was surprised to see the other three men standing there waiting, kind of like a welcome committee. But the real surprise was the scene behind them.

Billy could see now because there were lanterns all lit up. It was a big room in the old factory building's basement. It looked like a rooming house with cots, tables and chairs all around. There was even a couple of couches, which had seen a lot of use. And on one side, there was a little fire burning in another alcove with a pot hanging over it on a metal pole. One of the best smells Billy could imagine was emanating from that pot.

"Is that soup?" he muttered.

"Yep it's Monday, soup day," laughed Bob. "Ain't everyday soup day," someone else replied.

"If we're lucky," came another voice.

Bob picked up two bowls and gave one to Billy, then reached for a big ladle lying on the hearth. He put it in the pot and began filling his bowl. When he was done, he indicated Billy was to do the same. He turned away and sat down at the nearest table followed by the kid, and then by his other train companions. No one said anything, just gulped down the delicious soup. And then like magic, a loaf of bread appeared on the table. A pair of grimy hands reached for it and proceeded to tear it apart giving pieces to the others. That was nice. Billy didn't even mind the dirty hands. He grabbed his piece, dipped it into his bowl of soup and it disappeared in two minutes.

"Wow", thought Billy, this is so good. "But wait, wait," he said.

"What for, kid?" someone asked him.

Well, in a low embarrassed voice he answered, "We didn't say grace."

Then the laughter erupted. One of the guys poked the man beside him in his ribs and said,

"One thing, you gotta admit, this young'un is mighty funny!"

Billy was embarrassed but Bob spoke up for him. "Go ahead kid, it's your turn, go ahead and say it, and the rest of you, shut up!"

After Billy lowered his head and said, "Lord, thank you for this food." Then another voice was heard,

"See that prayer was kind of like him, short and sweet," Then the place erupted with laughter.

Billy thought, "Oh boy, someday, I'm going to grow up and beat some sense into you morons, except Bob, of course". But immediately, he felt ashamed of that thought; first blessing, and then boasting. "Sorry, God. Guess I still got a lot to learn".

After they finished eating, they stood up and one by one found an empty cot to lay down on. Some of them went out like a light. Even the talking around them didn't keep them awake. Riding those rails makes a body tired.

Also, filling it up with soup helped their slumber.

Hours later, Billy woke up to the sounds of talking.

He sat up and looked around. At one table there sat a bunch of sorry looking creatures. Smoke arose from over them and he heard a jingle like coins being shaken. He wondered what they were doing, he and decided to get up and go see.

Before he got to the table, he recognized the smell of cigars and wondered where they stole them from as most of them didn't look like they'd done an honest day's work in their life! Boy I gotta stop judging these people, sorry God! And weren't they his friends of a sort?

Billy continued on and found the little sounds were indeed coins. Pennies, nickels and dimes. Now where did that money come from? And look how they were spending it! On cards! Man, he was never going to understand these men! Even his friend Bob! Because at that moment he heard Bob say, "Raise you two bits!"

He watched the rest of them mutter and throw their cards down. Bob smiled and raked the money in. When he saw the kid he said, "You got any money?" "Like he would tell him, friend or no friend," thought Billy.

"Nope, don't have any," was his reply. "Well then does anyone want to stake him a little?" asked Bob. No one volunteered.

"Sorry kid, maybe later," said Bob. "But guess you can watch and learn, that won't cost you anything."

Billy stayed with the players for a couple of hours then decided his head was getting too full, so he got up and went to a cot and fell asleep.

Chapter Four

*T*he next morning when Billy awoke everyone else was still asleep. He looked around for something to eat but found nothing, so he decided to venture out into the street and see what he could find. If he could find a job to make some money, he wouldn't have to steal his food.

He headed back the way they had come last night and found the street where stores lined both sides. When he spotted the vegetable and fruit stand, he wanted to avoid seeing the man wearing an apron and crossed to the other side. Great, none of the people he saw was the apron man. Billy walked a few blocks and found nothing he was looking for.

"Maybe if I try a side street", he thought, and walked back a block before turning down a side street. No stores were there but he could hear some loud noises and followed the sounds to an interesting work sight. A group of men in coveralls with tools strapped around their waists were standing together and watching a huge machine ramming into a building. The bricks were flying everywhere.

One of the laborers noticed him and told him to get

back out of the way before he got hurt. Billy stepped back but was intrigued with the scene. When the machine was backed up and shut off, the laborers went in with wheelbarrows and started picking up the debris. He approached one of them and asked who he could see about a job. The man looked him over, kind of smiled, and pointed toward a small shack. It looked like an outhouse and the kid thought he was joking with him.

"I don't have to go to the toilet," he said.

"That's the office", he answered. So, Billy went over to the little outhouse looking office and found it was empty. He was standing there like a lost pup when a large man wearing a big dirty hardhat came up to him. Gruffly he asked,

"What do you want kid?"

"I'm looking for a job to earn some money", Billy said.

The man asked, "What do you know how to do?"

"Well, I can use a hammer and a saw or I'm strong too. I can help with the cleanup," he answered.

The man replied, "You don't look big enough to carry your weight," he laughed then at his own sense of humor and shook his head.

"Please Mister, just give me a chance. I really need some money," begged Billy. The man reached into his pocket, pulled out a quarter and gave it to him and said, "Get lost kid."

"If you only knew how lost I already am", he thought. Still the smart thing to do was leave them alone, so he did.

Sticking to the main street seemed the best idea so he retraced his steps and went down the next side street. There was nothing there but more broken-down buildings. Billy was just about to turn around and go back when he caught sight of some kids playing in front of one of the buildings. Wanting to observe the kids more closely, he walked close by the old building. But as he approached them, they stopped and stared at him.

He said "Hi" but they didn't answer, just started looking down at their feet. Billy didn't know what to do so he just stood there. Then when some woman started hollering out an upstairs window,

"You kids come in here," so now he knew people lived in these buildings.

Now what to do, wondered Billy. But just then he noticed another person coming around from the back of the building. It was a crippled boy, using crutches. At first Billy just stared at him and he stared back.

"Who are you?" the boy on crutches finally asked.

In spite of Billy's financial condition, he thought, "You poor boy". He didn't know if the boy lived in poverty but how thankful he was not to be like him.

"I'm Billy," he said. "What's your name?"

"My name's Rich. You're not from around here, at least I've never seen you before," spoke the kid looking up at Billy.

It was pitiful, him being bent over so bad only thing easy to see was his feet.

"What's wrong with your back and legs?", Billy asked, then silently wished he hadn't. He had no right to ask and could only pray he didn't offend him. Guess he wasn't offended, because he started laughing. That just bewildered Billy more and he wondered how the crippled boy could laugh about his condition. His back's been broken but his spirit sure hasn't. "Wow, this kid is really pretty awesome," he thought.

In a few minutes Rich settled down, and said,

"Don't feel sorry for me, ok? Now that would really make me mad! I get enough of that. Seems like I'm just an embarrassment to people. My Mom gets kind of nasty if she thinks someone's staring at me, as if they could help it," he laughed at himself.

"I'm not exactly like most other boys," Rich went on talking. "And guess what? I'm glad. No one expects me to do much. I suppose they think my mind's poorly too. Helps me fool them", he snickered, "especially at school. Don't have to study much and my teachers just keep passing me on. But that's enough about me, tell me what's up with you?"

Billy really didn't know what he should tell Rich. He didn't know how much he could trust him. He was a runaway and the last place he wanted to go was back to his home. And he didn't respect the law or even trust them. They never protected him or his mother. Seemed like the bad guys always won. Still he couldn't just stand there and say nothing, if he left now the other kid might get suspicious so he kind of told the truth.

"I'm traveling out west with my granddad," then chuckled to himself. Bet old Bob would love to know he just got himself a grandson.

"Well, where is he? And how are you traveling? Sorry but you look a little down and out."

"Now what do I say", thought Billy?

"Well, a terrible thing happened, my granddad fell stepping out of the train and ended up in the hospital. They have him strapped down with his leg in the air with a big bandage or cast they called it. Don't know when he's getting out of there."

"That's awful, where are you staying?" asked Rich.

"I'm kind of just hanging out in a place close to the hospital," he answered.

Then Rich inquired, "What kind of place, one without any water? Because you could stand to wash up."

Billy thought, "he'd better open up and tell Rich something he would believe".

"My folks are dead, and I have no other relatives except my granddad. And we're kind of short on money too, so I'm doing the best I can."

"I'm sorry," replied Rich and just felt he had to do something to help his newfound friend.

"Do you want to come home with me? I'm sure my mom won't mind. She's always taking in strays, mostly animals but one time she did bring a man home. Boy, she better stick to animals because that man stole all her money and even her wedding ring she'd hid away in the back of her dresser drawer. That really hurt because my dad got killed in the war and that was all she had to remember him by. That and a medal and a flag the army sent her. But she likes kids and is really sorry I don't have any brothers or sisters. So come on, we live just around the corner over the grocery store."

Billy walked with him back up the street, turned the corner and headed to his home. They got to the grocery store and luckily no one was out on the sidewalk. There was a door beside the big window. Crates and barrels of food were stacked near-by. Rich opened it and told Billy to come in. When Billy stepped inside, they were faced with a tall staircase.

"Now how is this poor guy going to make it up these stairs facing us", wondered Billy?

Again, Rich laughed as he looked at him. It was almost like he could read his mind.

"I can do it, climb these stairs I mean, it takes me a while, but I get there. The two handrails help a lot, follow me up."

Billy stood in awe watching him literally pull his whole body up the stairs. It was then Billy looked and saw how broad his shoulders were. *"No wonder"*, he figured. And he had put his arms through the top of the crutches bringing them up with him. His twisted legs were actually helping too. Billy tried not to stare but just think, it was only a couple of hours ago that he'd been feeling sorry for himself!

Finally, they reached the landing and Rich picked up the corner of a rug, pulled out a key and used it to open the door. Billy thought, "didn't they know that's the first place a burglar would look for a way into their place? But then again probably wasn't much in there worth the trouble of climbing the stairs and breaking in for."

Billy followed Rich inside and looked around. There wasn't a lot to see, but it did look clean and kind of homey. When he felt something furry wrap around his legs he jumped back.

"Ack, he shouted, what is it?" He looked down and saw not one but two big hairy cats rubbing against him.

"It's ok, that's just their way of saying hello and welcome. They're Pete and Repete; brothers or at least Mom found them in the alley together and they do sort of look alike.", Rich replied.

"Boy they're two of the ugliest cats I ever saw", Billy thought, but he didn't say anything because something else caught his attention. It was a big dog with only three legs. He was lying under the window and softly growling his welcome home. Billy didn't know what to think or feel. But he'd really be some watch dog to fear if he'd had all his legs!

"That's Triage", Rich said laughing softly and petting him. "Bet you can't figure out how he got that name." And then he said, "We get along real good, us old cripples. But he can beat me up and down those stairs, especially at nighttime after being locked in here all day because some days Mom doesn't have time to open up the bottom door during her lunch time helping me. Still most of the time I let him out when she can't."

"What a welcoming committee!", thought Billy, but he did say his mom was always taking in strays. Wonder if there's anymore? He looked around the room. Rich saw him and again read his mind.

"That's all we got right now, just buried old Spook,

Mom has a limit of four. That's all we can afford to feed. She's been real lucky finding homes for lots of other homeless pets. But she makes sure they get a good home. So, come on over and set a spell, Mom will be up pretty soon for lunch and she'll fix us something good."

Chapter Five

*T*rue to his word, it was only a 'short spell' before Billy heard her footsteps coming up the stairs. The door opened and Rich's mom stepped inside. Billy noticed she had blond hair and when she smiled at them, he thought she looked like an angel. Even more surprising than her looks was her name. When Rich told Billy his mom's name was Angela Gardner, Billy looked at her face again and thought it glowed.

"What do you have here son, a new friend?" she asked.

"Mom, this is Billy, he's passing through town with his grandpa but guess it's not been a good time since his grandpa is in the hospital.", said Rich.

"What's wrong with your grandpa, Billy" Angela asked.

"He broke his leg and hurt his back," Billy answered still looking at her angelic face. He wished he could have had a mom like her. Maybe if he was nice to her, she would keep him like the pets.

"You poor thing, do you have family or somebody to look after you here?" she asked.

"Well, I don't have any family, but I do know a few of my grandpa's friends," Billy replied.

When she asked where he was staying, he answered, "I'm just hanging around a couple of places."

It was then that Rich thought he'd better step in, before she actually discovered the truth.

"Mom, we sure are hungry."

She laughed, "When aren't you hungry? I'll go see what I can find."

After she went into another room Billy assumed was the kitchen, he looked at Rich and said, *"Thanks."*

Rich just smiled and shook his head, like yes or ok, then they both settled back on the couch.

A few minutes later a smell floated through the door that caused Billy's mouth to start watering. He thought, "I've never smelled anything so good". He was starved. He couldn't help himself and leaned forward toward the aroma causing Rich to burst out in laughter.

"Smells like some of her homemade chili, do you like chili?"

"Oh yeah, I sure do. When do you think it'll be ready? I'm hungrier than a hound dog.", said Billy.

"Should be any minute", Rich said, "because Mom's only got a half hour for lunch. But we are blessed because she not only works in the store below, but we live up here for free."

When she called and told them to come out to the kitchen, they raced each other. Billy won of course, since his opponent was handicapped.

Billy liked the kitchen. It was small, but neat and

clean and smelled so good, just right for two people. Only there were just two chairs at the small table. When he stopped short of the table and looked at her, she said,

"Go ahead Billy and take a seat," so he did.

He was so hungry he almost forgot and picked up his spoon to eat before saying grace. He knew better. Rich arrived leaning over and pulled out the other chair to set on before putting his crutches on the floor. Then when Billy lowered his head, Rich did likewise. Both waited to see who was going to pray. Finally, Rich's Mom said,

"Thank you, Father for this food. Amen."

Both boys picked up their spoons and dug in like they were racing again. She stood by the stove holding a small bowl and quickly ate hers too. Then she gave them both a refill.

"I'll see you tonight sweetie," she said and leaned over Rich to kiss him on his head. That touched Billy, almost as if she'd kissed him, too.

"Boy are you lucky", he thought, "wish I had a mom like that".

After she left, they finished their soup and then Rich asked Billy if he would get into a cupboard, pointing at one, and get out some cookies. When Billy opened the cupboard door, he couldn't stop staring at a plate holding some heavenly chocolate chip cookies. He thought Rich's mom must be an angel for sure.

"How many should I get for us?" Billy asked.

"Just bring the whole plate and get us two glasses off the sink for milk from the icebox." He did as Rich said and for once felt like he had a real home. He thought he could be happy living here and was thankful he met up with Rich.

After they finished eating, they went back into the living room and collapsed on the couch.

"Man, I've never had a meal like that. Your mom is great, her food smells and tastes like it came from heaven," said Billy.

"Yeah, she's great just like her cooking," replied Rich. Then a thought came to Billy and he wondered if "that's really what heaven smells like. Don't think it's the angels though, you probably can't eat them. Forgive me God, I'm so bad."

But Billy was kind of right, because that night, like angels, her meal did have wings too.

"It's fried chicken night," Rich exclaimed.

"Hope she makes us mashed potatoes and gravy, and biscuits. I think Mom's going to outdo herself tonight. Maybe she's trying to impress you. Now if you were an older fellow, I could understand that, but you're just a kid like me. Well, for whatever reason, you're going to really enjoy this. If you thought that chili was something, just wait."

Billy didn't know what to think, feel, or say. So, he didn't do anything but just sit there.

An eternity later, she called them to come on into the kitchen and on the table was the greatest meal he ever saw. There was fried chicken, mashed potatoes, gravy, biscuits, and a bowl of greenish little cabbages that Billy didn't know what to call.

But then Rich said, "Oh Mom, not brussels sprouts!"

"Yes, and you're going to eat at least five of them. They're good for you. I wish you liked vegetables better, but you will in time." Rich's mom replied.

She filled their plates and then pulled over a small barrel, turned it upside down and sat on it.

"Now, this is nice and since I'm finished working for the day, we can all enjoy a relaxing meal. Whose turn is it to say grace? Rich, how about you?"

He said "sure, and started 'thanking' God for the meal, the provider and cook, for his new friend, for their warm home, and for anything else good he forgot to say before. Then he started asking for things like, good health for all of them, safety out in this wicked world and enough money to live on".

Finally, when Billy couldn't take it any longer and was going crazy to get started eating that wonderful food, unthinking, said a loud "Amen!"

"Oh my, what did I do?", he thought looking up at Rich and then his mom.

They both were smiling! Then they broke out with a gush of laughter. His mom laughed so hard she put her hand over her mouth and the other one on her stomach. She muttered, "Rich, you little stinker, will you please stop your carrying on? Poor Billy, what you must think of us."

"I think you're great Mrs. Gardner, you too Rich, but I guess I owe you one.", replied Billy!

He'd already experienced his new friend's sense of humor which amazed him considering his physical handicap. Still his mind was fine, and he had a wonderful mother. He was loved very much and maybe, pondered Billy, love cures everything. Guess he'd have to wait and see.

After they finished eating, they all pitched in and cleaned up the kitchen. When they were finished, they took the dog out for a long walk. It was nice for Billy, knowing he had a home waiting for him as Rich's mom had invited him to spend the night. It almost felt like he belonged there. And this ended one of the best days of Billy's life.

Chapter Six

*T*he next morning, he woke up late. It felt eerie with no one else there. Rich, nor his mom were in the apartment. He was uncertain what he should do, but knew he had to get up and get dressed. After folding the bedding stuff, he took one last look around, everything was tidy, so he headed for the door. He was surprised to see a note pasted on it. Rich wrote and told him there was cereal, sugar and a bowl on the kitchen table. He knew where the milk was, so he was to eat up, and then go down to the store.

Well he did eat and then slowly made his way down the stairs. He wasn't anxious to meet the apron man again, so he just hung around outside trying to look like he belonged there. Rich must have been wondering where he was because he came out of the store looking for him.

"Hey, where you been? What are you doing out here?" he asked.

"Which one of your questions should I answer first? See I can be funny too." Billy said.

"Ok, you win" replied Rich, "now what'll we do?"

Billy didn't have the faintest idea. Rich asked him if he was going to see his grandpa. Thinking fast, he said "Yeah, but can I come back tomorrow, will you be busy?"

"Well I'll probably be able to fit you into my schedule," said Rich. He was still laughing as Billy walked away.

Now what am I going to do, he wondered? "Guess I'll go see Grandpa," he told Rich. The part he didn't say was, he wondered if Bob was still in town. He started walking back to the warehouse basement hotel room and while making his way there, he thought about how much better he felt. Spending time with a friend like Rich and a loving mom like Angela Gardner had helped cure his loneliness. Guess that home cooking helped too.

He went inside when he reached the building and started looking for Bob. What a rat hole! When he went down into the hole he found some more, only these rodents were playing poker. They seemed surprised to see him and stared at him,

"Where you been, kid?" one asked.

"I made a new friend and stayed with him last night." Billy said.

"Oh yeah," Slim said and turned back to the poker game.

"Well, go ahead, it's your turn," said one of his opponents.

Billy wouldn't get caught up in their game so immediately asked where Bob was.

"Wish we could tell you. He left early this morning and went looking for you. Never thought we'd see the day when ole' Bob would go looking for a stray."

"What'd you do kid, cast a spell on him?"

They all seemed to think that was funny because they all started to laugh around the table. He didn't think it was funny, so he turned, went up the ladder and headed for the door. He went outside and started down the street in another direction from where he'd just come.

Hours later, and miles it seemed, he was worn out but hadn't found his old friend. He wondered what his new friend was doing and couldn't help thinking about food as he hadn't eaten since morning. Billy wondered what Rich's mom would fix for supper and wished he could be there to enjoy it with them.

But he didn't go find out. Instead, he headed back to the warehouse hoping Bob was now there. He was there and really mad! For once, Billy wished he could have been in two places at the same time. He wasn't sorry he had spent the night with Rich, but he didn't feel right about making ole' Bob so upset.

"Where have you been? I've been looking all over for you!", Bob declared.

"Well, I met this kid yesterday and he took me home to meet his mom. You won't believe this, but they live over the grocery store where you guys stole that food. Fact is, his mom works there in the meat department."

"What a coincident! Did she give you any that

meat?" asked Bob. He had calmed down some now after seeing Billy was back and ok.

"Oh yeah, she made us chili and fried chicken." Billy replied.

Bob replied, "Well aren't you the lucky one! Too bad you didn't bring some back for us. Well, maybe you brought some good luck. Let's go back to the poker table," Bob ordered.

Billy thought, "Guess he is over his mad spell" because he started laughing. Then what really surprised Billy was when Bob put his arm around him and told him;

"We haven't any home cooking here but there's some stuff to make peanut butter sandwiches. Go make us a couple and bring me a beer. It's in that old chest over there," pointing it out.

Billy opened it and surprise! A bottle of root beer was there too. He asked whose it was, and Bob said, "Yours if you want it." That made him laugh! If he wanted it! Only wondered where it had come from; stolen it probably.

After they ate, Bob went back to the poker table and Billy went searching for a spot to sleep. He was tired, it'd been a long day. And he was surprised to find he missed Rich and his mom. Even those two dumb cats and Triangle or Trilogy or whatever he was called. Oh yeah, it's Triage.

The next morning, he found Bob sitting outside like he was waiting for him.

"You ready to get out of Dodge, cowboy?"

"What do you mean?" Billy asked.

"If you feel like traveling, I'm itching to get aboard and move on."

That surprised Billy as he thought they'd be around here for a while, at least till they got some traveling money. He wondered if Bob and the other men ever worked or just went along stealing their food. He hungered to see his friend Rich and his mom and get to know them better. What would they think if he didn't even go back and say goodbye?

Well, he couldn't help it, he had to reach his goal of golden California. He also realized he was lucky to have found a friend like Bob, who knew how to travel, and more importantly, how to survive. He'd better go with Bob.

"Ok," Billy replied. "I'm ready whenever you are, let's go."

"Ok, let's gather up our stuff and get moving before the train pulls out.", Bob insisted.

When they approached the train station Bob said, "There it is", and pointed toward the train. "We're in luck, don't see hardly anyone, so come on."

They went to the back side of the train, down the track always and then stepped over the tracks, turned the corner and snuck into the first car. It wasn't filled with crates, boxes or barrels, but with horses! And surprise, their traveling friends were filling up some spaces too.

As the train started moving, Slim said, "If that don't beat all, we're stuck in horse manure all night!"

The train picked up speed and they were on their way along with Slim and Simple. The three of them had been with them on the last train so, Billy couldn't help wondering about Sir, their other traveling companion. He hoped he wasn't in jail even though he probably deserved it.

"But look at the bright side", he thought, "three square meals a day, a bed, toilet, and no working, almost enough to make Billy jealous". But on the other hand, one couldn't do much traveling locked up in a small cell. "Oh no, not for me!", he thought.

"Well", thought Billy, "couldn't smell any worse than some of those old travelers did. Guess you wouldn't even need a pot, seeing if you'd mix your mess with the horse's mess who'd know the difference? And they'd be a lot quieter too, than grumpy men or worse yet, hung over old men."

As the train sped along, the men went thoughtlessly on their way. Billy seemed to be the only happy one among them. He wondered what Rich's mom was fixing them for supper and thinking about food made him hungry. Did the night with Rich and his mom spoil him or what? He wondered if anyone thought to bring food with them but didn't ask. He felt blessed to be on his way to the land of opportunity.

"Praise God!" He wanted to sing and shout like some of those black folks in church. Man, was he getting religious or what? Now that would surprise his old man, the one he left at home, not Bob. "Thank God, oops there I go again," as he laughed

"What are you laughing at now kid?" asked Slim. "You a horse lover or something? You might be now, but let's see how you feel in the morning."

"Just shut up, I got to get some sleep," Slim growled and headed over to the last stall where he pushed some straw together for a bed. He curled up in the corner and was quiet until Billy heard him snoring. He didn't know how they could sleep and cracked the door open to watch the world go by.

"Hey, kid, shut the door, you're letting the light in!" Slim hollered.

"Oh", he thought, "it was going to be a long day, or night, because it was so dark in there!" Billy knew he couldn't sleep as he was too excited about what kind of rousing adventures lay ahead.

Chapter Seven

Riding the rails as hobos, was always an adventure that kept a man on his toes and Billy's next surprise came early the very next morning. After a long restless time, his mind went into the shut-down mode that gave him sleep for a short time. He awoke to find his rested travelers in the process of leaving the train's horse stable. Bob said, "Come On." He didn't know what was happening but, grabbing his few possessions leaped through the door after them.

They went toward town walking together and laughing as if they didn't have a care in the world; As if they hadn't just missed being found on the train and possibly arrested. As they walked, they came to a church and went around the building ending up in a graveyard.

"Wow!" exclaimed Billy. "What a place for us to get some rest because there's a lot of folks here getting theirs, and it still looks like there's plenty of space for us." He laughed but no one else did. Then he asked; "What's the matter guys, why the long faces?"

"Well, funny boy, guess you didn't hear the two men

open that train door, then after looking in, one of them told the other man the horses had arrived and they had to go get help to unload them," Slim replied.

"No, I didn't," Billy said, "So what's next?"

Bob reached out and patted him on the head, "Ok, settle down, all of you! Slim, go back to that gas station we just passed and get us some coffee. I've got some bread and peanut butter. That'll be enough for now. Hopefully another train will come by soon."

Slim returned in a short while with coffee for the men and a cup of milk for Billy.

"Thanks, Slim, that was awful nice of you," he said. Bob's laughter at Billy's expression caused him to stop and ask,

"What's the matter Bob? I did thank him."

"You used two ordinary words together with opposite meaning, 'awful' and 'nice'," Bob explained. I've heard that's called an oxymoron, can't you make up your mind whether Slim is awful or nice?"

The rest of the gang started laughing then too and so did Billy. "I get it, ok?" he said, shaking his head with bright red cheeks.

They settled down then and ate their breakfast. But after resting a while Slim said,

"Alright, guys let's hit the trail, case the preacher man decides to come to his job. Let's see what this town has to offer."

Billy thought to himself, "what he actually meant was what they could help themselves too. He recalled the old saying he'd learned, 'God helps them who help themselves' or something like that and wondered if that was what Slim was thinking."

They divided up into two groups, the two (B's) Bob and Billy and the two (S's) Slim and Simple formed the second. They turned and walked away in opposite directions.

"Let's go back to that gas station because it's the closest and we did buy something from there," said Slim. They caught a break there, as they entered the attendant stepped outside for his break then went over to pump gas for some lady who seemed uncertain how to pump or how much she could afford.

The two men put a few items in their pockets and under their shirts, then started out the door as the attendant and lady were coming in. He said, "I'll be with you guys in a minute."

Slim replied, "No, that's ok, I didn't find anything I really want." His pal basically gave the same excuse as they proceeded outside smirking at each other. They hurried on down the sidewalk to explore other opportunities.

Bob took Billy and headed for the center of town. There, they discovered a large statue of a man standing in the middle of a round pool of water with a bunch of coins in it.

Bob said, "Either there's a lot of fools with a lot of money or a bunch of dreamers expecting to get their dreams to become realities."

Billy laughed and said, "Hope our guys don't see this because they'll be taking those peoples dreams out of this place come dark time." He also thought but didn't say it out loud, "I don't want these coins because I'm going to find gold when I get to good ole' California".

As the darkness of night settled over the town and the group reunited at the old church yard, Slim was first to think about what possibilities the building held.

"Wonder if this preacher is a trusting man? Let's see if he locked up the building?"

When he tried the back door it swung open, "Come on guys, let's go inside and see what's here." Slim said.

They followed him inside and found a restroom on the left side with a kitchen on the right. "Any of you have to use the bathroom? I'm gonna check out this kitchen. After all isn't God supposed to feed us and we're supposed to feed on the word of God, right guys?"

They all laughed and went into the kitchen. They opened the small fridge and then the cabinets. Even though they were stealing from God's people, God still blessed them when they found quite a few cans of soup and tuna fish. Jars of peanut butter and jelly along with crackers and a couple loaves of bread made a good stash.

Slim asked, "Did any of you notice what kind of church this is, because I'm thinking it must be Baptist because they're noted for their eating events along with their religion, right Billy?"

The naive youngster just shook his head in disbelief at Slim's ignorance. "Well, maybe you can make this right, there's probably a contribution plate out there in the sanctuary, case you found some coins in that fountain!" Billy said. "What fountain," asked Slim?

Bob interrupted and said, "Never mind, let's eat, and Billy this is another chance to make us say grace."

Simple said, "I vote for soup, that 'two-burner' over there will heat it up." They all started asking each other what kind they should eat until Slim erupted,

"Man, let's eat that chicken soup, who knows, might keep us from getting down with a cold, or worse the flu."

"Buddy, I think you're a bit confused, putting the cart before the horse. You eat that soup not to prevent but to cure a cold, understand?" Bob exclaimed or should one say, explained.

After finishing their dinner, they decided to sleep on the pews which luckily had padded seats. Bob reminded them to wake up early to give them time to eat breakfast before the preacher came to work. "So, use the bathroom and wash up some while there's still enough moonlight to see around," he advised.

Chapter Eight

*T*he next morning Bob woke them up just as the sun was waking up.

"Let's grab a bite to eat and get out of here while the getting is good."

They grumbled but did as he said and headed back into town. Then he said,

"I don't know why we didn't go to the train station yesterday and see when the next ride is coming in and where they're heading, hopefully west. They usually have it posted you know. Me and the kid will do it because the rest of you smelly bums would just call unwanted attention to us. Cause it doesn't seem like you washed up too good last night!"

Bob and Billy walked to the train station and found the next train wasn't in until evening and would be headed to El Paso. When they reported to the others,

Slim said, "It'll nearly be dark by that time and gettin' aboard should be easy, right?"

They all agreed and since they had all day to kill, they split up to look around town and see what more it had to offer. The split was the same way as the day before.

The guys met again around six o'clock and when all were present Bob said "Ok, follow me."

They went around the rear end of the caboose to the opposite side of the cars. A quick stop and look around told them that no one was in sight, so Bob said,

"Ok, whose turn to choose?"

"Could I?" Billy asked.

"Oh no, young'un, I'm afraid you haven't enough experience yet. Look how you found us," Bob answered.

The other men started a low chain of laughter, then Slim said, "Hush you stupid bums, do you want someone to hear us?"

"Bum?" erupted Bob, "but then, I guess as the old saying goes 'Takes one to know one' and that's probably why we get along so well." Slim reached out and lightly punched him in the belly.

"Well, are you, grownups done horsing around, and speaking of horses, hope we don't find any more of them," said Billy.

Then Bob, their self-appointed leader said, "Let's check out these first cars, and make it fast because you know this here train's not going to set here forever."

They strung out along the cars and the last two in line, Simple and Slim, stopped at the last door. Then Bob took Billy's arm and went ahead of them to the next car. Slim was so tall he was able to reach up and slide the door open then climb inside. After crawling in, he then reached down and pulled his buddy up inside the boxcar.

Bob got down on his knee, Billy climbed up and managed to slide the door open.

"Look around," Bob said. "And see if you can find anything I can use to step up on."

Billy looked up along the track and found a large paint bucket which worked perfectly. Bob set it on the ground and climbed in then he helped Billy. He held Billy's legs as he retrieved the bucket then patted Billy on his shoulder,

"Good job partner," he said. "You should have seen me trying to get on when I first climbed on this train. It took a lot of huffing and puffing but I managed to do it."

It only took about ten minutes to look inside the cars then Slim and Simple joined Bob in a huddle, reporting what was in their car. The team of Slim and Simple said their car just had some crates, not much for us to sleep on.

"There's a bunch of machinery and crates in this one too", Bob said. "It's not much to look forward to but it'll probably work. Me and the kid will take this car and you guys can take the other one, are we in agreement?"

They looked at each other, put out their right hands and nodded yes. Then Slim and Simple returned to their car.

Lucky for all of them, there was still a bit of daylight time so they could find their resting spot. Of course, they all carried flashlights except for young Billy. They didn't use them much because they didn't know how much juice their batteries had. They no sooner had the doors shut when they heard the engineer crank up the engine.

Billy asked, "Bob, how long will it take us to reach El Paso?"

"Should be about twenty hours is my estimation," he answered.

"Or your guess-ta-mation," Billy said with a frown. "Do you mean we have to stay in this place for a whole day?" He was anxious about the time.

"Well you just never know. A lot of things could happen, like us getting caught, the engine breaks down, a collision with another train, or maybe we fall off the track and tumble down an incline. But for now, please stop with the questions and let's get settled, I need some rest. Ok buddy?" answered Bob.

They settled down then but in a short time their peace was interrupted by a sobbing cry. They both looked at each other and Bob shrugged his shoulders indifferently then shook his head. Billy couldn't help it, he wanted to respond.

"Hello, where and who are you?" he asked.

"I'm over here in the corner."

"Which corner?" Asked the perplexed boy.

"I don't know but I'll stand up, please don't hurt me," was the reply.

There was a big box that a skinny looking kid stepped around as Bob flashed his flashlight on him. The boy looked around Billy's age and was holding his head down to shield his face.

"It's ok kid, we won't hurt you," Billy answered and then asked,

"How did you get in here and when?"

"Just a little while before you did. I heard you guys open the door, so I hid behind this big box full of some kind of machinery," the boy answered.

Bob said, "Young'un, I don't think it's equipped to hide you."

Then the new one shyly said, "I have to go to the bathroom."

"Sorry kid, this room doesn't have that facility. Now, what's your name?" Bob inquired.

"Call me Lane."

"Well Lane, I hate to disappoint you but just try and hold it as long as you can."

"I can't hold it in much longer, please tell me what to do," he desperately answered.

"Well, you're lucky because we can slide the door open and you can do it the way us fellows do," said his new leader.

"I gotta do number two," he cried out.

Billy looked at Bob and asked, "Could he use the paint can we got?"

"Sure, give it to him and kid, take it with you, hopefully there's enough space in your corner for the bucket. If that box isn't too heavy, maybe we can pull it out some. Get behind there and see," Bob told the new kid.

The kid squeezed back into his corner then said, "I need a little more space, I'll push this corner and maybe you guys can pull it out for me."

The kid was grateful because the team effort worked. And Billy remembered he had some toilet paper, that is, a Sear's and Roebuck catalog, which he threw over the top of the new bathroom.

Then he thought, "Please Lord, don't let him stink up our new home too much".

The Lord rewarded them for their acts of kindness, as they couldn't smell much, well maybe a little. Thankfully, neither of them had to use the new toilet in the corner.

So, the day ended on a positive note as the train's motion lauded them into a good night's sleep.

Chapter Nine

*I*n the middle of the night when the train was coming to a stop, Lane woke them up.

"What's happening, he wanted to know, and why are we stopping?"

"I don't know," Bob answered. "Billy, slide that door open and see what's going on."

Billy did as Bob said and peeked out but didn't see any reason for the train to stop.

"I gotta take a leak, anyone else need to go?"

"No, I'm good for now," replied Bob.

"How about you, Lane?"

"I don't need to do that, but I think I might use the can again, guess I didn't get finished last night," Lane replied.

"I think I could hear you," Bob said. "Or then again, maybe I was just dreaming."

"Yeah, you were dreaming because I could hear you snoring and mumbling about something. Sometimes I could make out your mumbling, something about a new home in California. Reckon someone has one waiting for you?" teased Billy.

Bob didn't answer and the rest of the night flew by even though it was a train, not a plane. It was barely daylight when the train came to a stop again and Bob slid the door open. He saw the engineer jump down out of the locomotive with a big bag slung over his shoulder.

"Well kids, we're in luck. I just saw the engineer leave the train carrying his bag, so my guess is he's on his way into town for some sleep. We may be picking up some more travelers tomorrow, hopefully the ones who bought a ticket and not any more like us who are looking for a free pass." Bob said.

He spoke with a concerned look toward his two young traveling companions and hoped they both safely would get to where they were going.

"Speaking of travelers, let's go and notify the other men of what's happening," he told Billy.

They went to the car holding them and he knocked on the door, but no one answered. Perplexed he pounded louder and again waited. He was about to move on when he heard a sleepy sounding voice whisper,

"What?"

"That was Slim," Bob told the others.

"It's Bob, open the door, we have another traveler I want you to meet."

Slowly the door slid open. "All of you come on down," Slim said.

They did but Simple looked like he might take off running any time. Bob pointed toward Lane who was just visible in the morning light.

"Oh great," uttered Slim, "just what we need, another kid! Guess you got your work cut out for you ole' boy. What are you anyway, some kind of saint or just a plain ole' caretaker? Does the kid have some money we can use?"

Bob continued, "Why don't you all shut up a minute, I've got something important to tell you? All the passengers seemed to have gotten off and then the engineer got off carrying his overnight bag so we're here for the day. You've got all day to check the town out. I suggest we all come back and sleep here tonight since you might not have the chance to get aboard in the daylight."

"What's this town called, Bob?" asked Lane.

He reached into his traveling bag and brought out a map he opened and studied it for a few minutes. Then pointed out a place,

"I'd say it was a pretty good chance of being the biggest one, El Paso", said Bob and he pointed it out to them on the map.

Billy said, "Let's go find something to eat, I'm starving for some good eats, something home cooked."

"Me, too," said the other young partner.

"Ok but who's buying, are you, Lane?" Bob looked from one young face to the other. "I'm sorry but I don't have much money on me," he apologized.

"Bob, we'll donate a couple of bucks. If you can too and we don't get greedy, we can at least get some soup, or better yet, split a dinner!" volunteered Billy.

"That's generous of you, young'uns but you'll have

to hold on to that appetite till no one is around to see us leave our home," he cautioned them.

The other two didn't think much of his idea and looked a little down in the mouth. Their clothes and hair all looked pretty messy too, and Bob told them the first place they needed to go was to the bathroom in the station to clean themselves up.

"Do the best you can before we go find a restaurant, we don't want to look like hoodlums," Bob told them.

Billy knew they were lucky to have a smart and experienced traveling friend like Bob. And then he said a silent prayer thanking God for the best traveling companion in the world. He also prayed someday he could pay him back. Little did he know how this would occur in their future!

They split up as usual and Bob took the kids with him as prearranged. Slim and Simple shuffled off together eager to find something they could pick up. None of them had but a few coins so buying their supper was not an option.

The tracks and station were located up on a hill and when the evening lights came on, they were speechless. When they looked down and saw all the lights, Lane said,

"Wow! It looks like this town is filled with stars."

"I agree," Billy said. "I never saw anything like this before. Bob, how do we know what direction to take?"

"It'll be alright, just stay close to me." Bob pointed toward town and said, "Let's go down this center street, at least I think it's the center."

They passed a lot of stores and some weren't open while others were. Every time they came to some kind of restaurant, the hungry kids looked hopefully at Bob who would shake his head and motion for them to move on.

Finally, when it seemed they had passed all the restaurants, he stopped and pointed at a church with a long line of sorry looking people standing in line. Billy wondered why he was pointing at them and then saw a sign which invited everyone in for a meal.

It wasn't a Baptist church this time but a Lutheran church. It didn't seem to matter to Bob who joined in the line and the kids followed. Billy knew it would be within their budget as it was most likely free.

"Hallelujah!" thought Billy, "I guess it's another chance to be thankful to the 'Great Provider' for yet another of His blessings".

A second prayer was that the line would move fast. The first smell of food caused his belly to start grumbling as he thought, "Feed me, Lord, and feed me now!"

Lane's stomach must have been answering Billy's, at least he imagined he could hear it. He didn't tell Lane though as he was afraid that he might laugh or maybe think he was crazy, in other words.

"Keep your mouth shut even if you can't make your stomach keep quiet," Bob cautioned.

It actually only took about ten minutes and they couldn't believe their eyes. There were three lines of tables with every imaginable kind of food and plenty of it was still left for them. Bob motioned for the two of them to come around front of him which they did. They picked up a plate and immediately started piling food on it. After waiting all day to eat, they felt starved and started eating from their plate.

"Wait till we get to a place to sit down," Bob told them. "And then eat there, not in line!"

The kids thought that was one of, if not the worse kind of advice they'd ever heard. They looked at Bob and his eyes told them to comply, then pointed them to a line of tables with chairs.

After getting seated, immediately they started cramming their mouths full only to have their leader hand signal them to stop. They looked at each other and Bob asked,

"Whose turn is it to say grace?"

"What's grace?" asked Lane.

"It's when you offer up a prayer of thanks to the Lord. Didn't you know that?" inquired Billy.

"No, we never prayed and living with my mean old step-dad, didn't make me thankful for anything. Finally, getting away from him is about the only thing I have to be thankful for, except for meeting you two guys," Lane stated.

"Well we're glad God led you to us, right, Bob?" For once Billy felt at home with Bob.

"Ok, you two, I'd be mighty thankful to be able to eat now, fact is I'm volunteering to do grace right now."

He proceeded to thank the Savior for the train ride, for all his friends, especially for the two young'uns.

Then when Billy interrupted with, "Thank you for this food, Amen!" Bob laughed and started joining them in eating really fast.

The rest of their time seemed to fly by. They enjoyed the people, the way they dressed and the slow draw of their voices. Billy made the comment how he saw in the cowboy movies a lot of gun fights and said, "I reckon they're lucky!"

Lane asked, "What are you talking about?"

"Well if the cowboys had drawn their guns as slow as these people talk, there would probably be a lot more live ones," Billy explained.

"You know how lucky you are, Bob? I don't mean at cards, but to have friends. You have such a great sense of humor, always making people see what's going on as something funny." Billy told him.

"I think that's why we get along so well because you youngsters seem to laugh a lot in life. Your past and present don't seem too uplifting. And speaking of uplifting, I think it's about time we high tailed it back to our temporary residence where I'll have to lift the two of you up through the door. Thank God for the bucket because you sure can't lift me up, even if both of you tried to do it together." He reached out and hugged them.

"And we might get even luckier if there's a faucet on the outside of the station where we can rinse out your toilet."

Billy couldn't help but think how lucky they were to have him, not only for his sense of humor but also his experience, knowledge and wisdom. And how blessed to have someone who seemed to care for him as the only one he ever had to love him was his mom.

"Do you reckon the other men will be settled in?" asked Billy.

"The only thing we can hope for is they stayed sober enough to find their way back home to the train," Bob replied.

Billy didn't know yet, but the three S's had gotten into a fight with some drunken locals. They were all under the influence, in fact, the home boys were just as guilty. But they were the visiting team and because the bar tender didn't want to lose his regular customers, he had lied to the police. But before they got there, Slim and Simple used their head and got out of there. But poor Sir didn't and thus ended up in jail.

Chapter Ten

*B*ob and the kids slept little that night. But considering how hard their beds were and they only had a few items of clothing for pillows, it could have been worse. They awoke when the train started moving and blowing the horn calling out a "Good morning" to them and saying "Goodbye" to Slim and Simple who had decided to stay in that town where Sir was in jail, at least until he got out.

Lane stood up and Billy saw a bright red spot on the backside of his pants. After pointing it out to Bob he raised his eyes and said to Lane,

"Either you set in some blood or you're bleeding, what's going on?"

"Good grief child, are you a girl?" asked Bob

He or she started crying, "Yes, but what's happening to me, how do I stop this? I don't want to bleed to death!"

"Lane, don't you know what's happening?" Bob asked.

"No," she cried out even louder.

"It's your monthly, it's what happens to a young girl when they become a woman," he told her.

"What's a monthly?" asked Billy."

"Never mind for now."

"Young lady, don't you realize how unsafe it could be for a girl to be traveling with a bunch of unlikely characters on a train?" the old gentleman was both surprised and stunned.

"Yes Sir, that's why I cut my hair and pretended to be a boy. Promise me you guys won't tell anyone," pleaded the frightened young lady.

"It's ok sweetheart, you're safe with us, right Billy?" he assured her.

"Yes sir, don't worry Lane, we'll protect you if need be. But I do have question, what's your real name?" Billy asked Lane.

"My name is Caitlyn. I was going to just use the last bit, but I didn't think Lynn would sound right for a boy, so I decided on Lane, because Lane kind of rhymed with Lynn. What do you think?" she asked.

Billy thought for a minute then said, "Sure, I think that's good. What do you think, Bob?"

"I don't think you need to worry about a name right now. I think Caitlyn needs to go over in the corner and take off her pants then set on the bucket a while. I hope you have another pair of pants to put on." Bob asked.

"I do," she answered.

"Try to get yourself cleaned up then use these two handkerchiefs of mine to keep it from getting on your clothes again. Do you have an undershirt that could be used until we can get you the real things to use?" Bob inquired.

"I've got one," Billy said, opening his backpack. He pulled it out and gave it to Caitlyn. She thanked him but looked downward all the time, embarrassed to meet his eyes.

"The train won't be stopping until we reach Tucson and that will be most of the day, so you have time to take care of yourself. That'll have to do till we can get you some pads in the closest store we see," Bob told her.

"The next best thing would be if you've got the money to pay for them," he added.

"Yes Sir, I do. In fact, Mom taught me to save my allowance. Bless her heart."

Billy scowled, "That's something we have in common. I have a good blessed mom, too. And another thing, I don't have much money either. How about you Bob, you are our stand in dad?" He looked hopefully at Bob but didn't expect he had much money either.

"Well kid, I do have a little money. You didn't know it, but I was luckier than you thought at cards," he informed him.

They all settled down for the day after it was Lane or Caitlyn's misfortune to reveal her true identity. Finally, after waiting all day they heard the train slowing down. Bob quietly slid the door open and stuck his head out to see what was happening. When the train came to a stop, he opened it further and signaled the kids to line up behind him. What amused him was that Billy had his stepdown bucket in hand but was holding it out at arm's length to keep from seeing its contents.

181

"Thanks for remembering", Bob said, "but don't hold it too close, because it kind of stinks."

Billy hoisted on his backpack then told Bob,

"I'll hop out first and empty this bucket so you can use it to step down on."

Billy jumped down onto the ground and found a place to empty the toilet bucket then turned it over for Bob to slide out and down onto. He handed it back up to Caitlyn who put it back in the corner.

She went to the doorway then, and Bob and Billy lifted her out and down before sliding the door shut behind her.

They walked up to the station to check the train schedule and Bob noticed a few people were already sitting outside on benches waiting for the next train. They went inside to check the posted train schedule and found out a train would be pulling out in just another hour and fifteen minutes.

Bob said, "Come on kids we need to hurry and see if we can find a place to buy the needed sanitary pads for Caitlyn."

They were in luck. A grocery store was just a short distance away. They went in and bought the pads and a belt, a loaf of bread, some baloney, chips, bananas, and a bottle of orange juice. Bob asked the store lady if she would take Caitlyn to their bathroom and help her. When Caitlyn came back, they hurried to the train hoping no one was close enough to see them sneak back aboard.

Bob said, "Just sit back and relax. The train should

be pulling out real soon then we can pig out with our picnic. And guess what, I nominate Caitlyn to say grace. Ok, young lady?"

"Yes Sir," she replied.

"And something else kids, on the bulletin board I saw the destination of this train is not San Francisco but San Diego. But I'm sure we'll find another train going that way. So, for now, as the engineer is starting to do his job and we're on our way to San Diego, let's dive into our scrumptious food."

"Great," said Billy. "I'm about starved to death."

"Young man, when aren't you hungry? But then again, you're at that age when you eat enough for two, kind of like your mom did when she was carrying you," laughed Bob. Caitlyn joined in too.

Billy's face turned rosy red as he shook his head, "I'll try to hold back as much as I can but I'm not promising anything because the two of you seem to be awful slow at eating. I wish you would hurry up and say grace, Caitlyn."

"Ok smarty pants, I'll show you I can talk fast. Lord, we thank you for this food, Amen."

Bob opened the loaf of bread, took out two slices and passed the loaf on to Caitlyn who took out two slices then gave it to Billy. Bob smiled at Caitlyn as he passed her the meat, chips and bananas. After they finished, Bob passed around the bottle of orange juice which caused Caitlyn to comment,

"I'm sure glad I'm next in line because it'd be empty if Billy got it first."

"Funny Caitlyn, but seriously I sure wish I had some of the raisin cookies my mom used to make for us," Billy said.

They finished their meal, then, as much as their circumstances allowed, stretched out to relax. Of course, the old fellow took his mini nap and the two young'uns softly conversed. A couple of hours later they could tell the moon was bright and slid the door open a little letting in some light. Bob surprised them when he asked,

"Would you like to learn how to play poker?"

"Yes, yes," Caitlyn cried out.

Billy said, "Well, I do know a little because of the times I watched you and the other guys. Still I sure would like to know more."

The teacher pulled out a pack of well-worn cards and began to teach his excited, young students.

"First, dig into your pockets and get out some playing change." Bob instructed. Billy and Caitlyn both had a little bit in a pocket, enough to get started.

They played cards or one might say, gambled for a couple of hours till the darkness of night turned off its light. The two kids were glad in one way as Bob was winning their money. But in another way not glad because as Billy told Caitlyn,

"No one's luck lasts forever," figuring they're luck should be waking up about the time they stopped.

Bob had to contemplate, if actually teaching them this new trade was such a good idea when he heard Billy's remark spoken in a sarcastic manner.

"Ok kids, he said, "I'm sorry to take your money. I'll give it back to you on one condition, that you'll never play poker again. Do you agree to my terms?"

"I'm sorry Bob, for being such a poor looser or maybe I should say a poor student," Billy said.

Caitlin added, "I'm sorry too Bob, its ok, you don't have to give me back my money, in fact I'm not even sure how much it was. But still I promise to never play poker again."

Then she added, "Life's hard enough without making it harder and I know you can get hooked on it like my Uncle June did. He lost their home because he was always playing cards at the local bar with his buddies. At least he thought they were friends. But in the end, when he couldn't make the house payments and the bank was threatening to take it not one of them was willing to help him keep it."

"Then my Aunt Sophie and the three little kids had to find somewhere to live. Luckily for them, our grandparents let them move in and when both of them finally died, Uncle Dave ended up inheriting their home. My cousin, Ruth, told me this right before I ran away, hopefully Uncle Dave learned his lesson!"

"That's good Caitlyn, what about you Billy?" Bob asked.

"Well I guess you better keep my money because I don't know if I can promise to not ever play poker again, I'm sorry." Billy apologized but couldn't look either in the eye.

"Well, I guess that's it then," Bob said. "I'm going to turn in for the night. Good night kids."

The other two found their spots and went down and out pretty fast as the old train rocked them asleep. The other travelers were blessed because they had places softer for sleeping. Some had soft seats and the best paying ones, actually had beds.

They awakened at dawn as the train came to a stop and Caitlyn asked,

"Why are we stopping, it's still nighttime isn't it? She was thinking, "But maybe not, the way my stomach is rumbling."

Bob sat up and listened, "No kid, its morning. Just wait a minute, I'll check."

He arose and went over to the door to slide it open. It allowed him to stick his head out and in the dim light, he could see a train station up ahead.

"Just as I thought, we are pulling into a station."

"I hope this doesn't take too long because I need to do my part for Mother Nature," Billy told them.

"What do you mean Billy?" asked Caitlyn.

"Isn't it a little early for jokes or are you practicing being a comedian if this gold thing doesn't pan out?" interjected Bob.

"Now who's trying to be the funny maker? I want to be the money maker. Now laugh on that bit of wisdom I'm giving to you, Mister Bob!" his young opponent returned.

"Please guys don't keep on going with this. We're all just trying to get to California, right?" said the emotional young girl who was experiencing the first step in becoming a fruit-bearing woman. She didn't really understand that a monthly time indicated she could now enter the realm of possible motherhood, even though it might take a while.

Bob made them peanut butter and jelly sandwiches, then reached into his magic bag and pulled out three candy bars. After handing one to each of them, he said,

"Unfortunately, kids, I don't have any more food. This is it until we stop long enough to get some more so, you might want to hang on to those candy bars until later. We should be pulling into our final destination in the morning and then we'll find us a place to really pack it in. Are you with me?"

Billy thought, "We really don't have much choice, do we?" But then replied, "Yeah, its ok, right, Caitlyn?"

"Yes, we'll make it fine, well maybe not fine but it'll probably help us appreciate our next meal," she answered.

It wasn't long before they continued, on what seemed a never-ending ride down the tracks. Billy and Bob shook hands then took turns standing at the cracked doorway for relief while Caitlyn went to do the same in her potty corner. They all laid back down then for the rest of the day as if it were still nighttime.

Toward evening they woke each other up feeling refreshed and yes, plenty hungry. They dug into the peanut butter and jelly jars but found very little. One banana was left, and Bob surprised them by digging out two apples he'd stored away. He gave one to Billy and cut the other one in two to share with Caitlyn.

Billy's stomach still crumbled with hunger that made him think about home, so he said, "Boy, I can't help thinking of the scrambled eggs or better yet, the pancakes and maple syrup mom used to fix for us."

"You're lucky! Mostly, all I had to eat was cold cereal which I had to hurry through, and then clean up the dishes before I could go to school", Caitlin added.

"Poor kid," Bob thought, as he shook his head.

Chapter Eleven

For Billy and Caitlyn, the rest of the evening and night seemed to drag on forever. It didn't bother Bob like it did the younger pair. He had spent most of his life riding in closed-up railroad cars, hours like these were just part of life. He took his usual fifteen-minute nap then was awake until darkness set in. He seemed at perfect peace drifting off into sleep as total darkness overtook the clickity clack of the train.

Billy asked Caitlyn if she'd like to play a game he made up. He called it twenty questions. They would each ask ten questions taking turns and she agreed. He started by asking her what she intended to do with the gold they found.

She answered, "First of all, how do you know we'll even find any?"

"Is that one of your questions, if it is you only have nine left?" Billy was saying when she answered, "Yes!".

He came back with, "Where's your faith? You gotta believe we can do this. The Bible says that God will provide and show you the way."

She came back quickly with, "How about your daily

prayer when you say to God, 'Give us this day our daily bread' and he isn't even doing that much? Bob provides more than God," she scoffed at him.

"Well, more important, at least for your sake, it also says, 'God will forgive my trespasses as I forgive those who trespass against me, so I guess I don't have any choice, I gotta forgive your wise cracks, smarty pants," he replied back.

"Ok, you've made your point. But I'm already getting a little bored with this, how about I teach you a game I've made up?" Caitlyn said.

He nodded his head and said, "Ok, go ahead."

"It's a card game," she announced

"No cards," objected Billy.

"This isn't a gambling game! What's the matter with you, she asked? I said I made up a new card game. How can I teach you a game you've already played and know about?"

"Sorry, Caitlyn go ahead, teach me," he apologized, kindly.

She didn't answer, just spread the deck out on the floor between them and told him to pick one and then she would pick one. He turned up a jack and she turned up an eight. She shoved the deck to him and said, "The highest one deals first."

He shoved them back to her saying,

"Well, that would be nice but you're the one who volunteered to teach me a new game. So, shuffle them up and get started showing me," he said with a mock sneer.

She shook her head in disbelief and said,

"Ok, step one, close your mouth and open your ears."

He demonstrated his zipper movement across his mouth, and she shot him a dirty look. She proceeded to shuffle the deck of cards then when finished offered it to him.

"Do you want to cut them?" Caitlyn asked

"Sure, why not, just in case you've learned to stack the deck," he teased.

"What a smarty pants you can be," she returned, then said,

"First, we deal out all the cards then you turn your first one up and then me, the highest card wins each pair. At the end, the one with the most cards wins the game. The loser has to cough up some dough, and not bread or cookie dough, real money."

Then she added, "How much do you think we should play for? What would you be willing to settle for, if, heaven forbid, you had beginner's luck and beat your teacher?"

"Well, let me think, oh I know, how about a piece of that Hershey bar I saw you take from the grocery store where we got your 'security' pads," Billy snorted out. Caitlyn just looked at him and said, "What are you talking about? I didn't steal anything there!" she declared.

"Oh yeah! Go get your shoulder bag," he retaliated.

"Ok, look, let's just get on with the game. The winner has the right to determine the prize," she declared.

Then Billy replied, "Ok, let's do it, you're starting to bore me, and I don't want to join the old man in his sleep time yet, so here goes!"

She dealt out the cards and they threw themselves into it. Billy wanted to keep the score on a brown paper grocery sack Bob always saved to make notes on. So, he said,

"Let's keep score! Bob's accumulated quite a stack of grocery sacks. I don't think he will miss one."

Billy deducted, he was actually writing something, like a story, but that was his old partner's privilege, so he never asked him. Caitlyn felt Billy didn't trust her enough to keep score, so she agreed to let him be scorekeeper.

They played for at least an hour before their talking awoke Bob. He watched them, then only inquired what kind of game it was and inwardly was glad it wasn't that addicting game of poker.

Ironically, just as he was having that thought, Caitlyn spoke up,

"We aren't playing that game of poker, Sir. Remember I promised not to play it again?"

Billy added, "It's one Caitlyn made up and is teaching me. But the winner does get something, we just can't figure out what it will be. Can you come up with an idea?"

"How about the loser has to clean up all the clutter every day for a week?" Bob suggested.

"Hey, sounds like a good idea, anyway I'm getting tired of picking up after Billy," said Caitlyn.

"What're you talking about? Since when, do you pick up anything except from the store?" replied Billy.

Caitlyn cried out, "Bob, he's such a liar! Have you ever seen me steal anything from a store?"

He replied, "No, frankly I haven't. But I have seen you pick up fruit that's fallen from a tree. Does that count?" Bob laughed.

Billy spoke before Caitlyn could and said, "I think that's just Mother Nature providing."

"Billy, you told me before, that it's God who provides," she said.

"Bob, I guess she is learning something from our discussions. Caitlyn, do you remember who created the trees so they could provide food for all mankind, and womankind too?"

"You know what Billy? You can be such a smart aleck, especially for someone so dumb!" she retaliated.

Bob interrupted, "You'll have to figure this out later, can you feel the train slowing down? And here comes the whistle. It must be water time as it's been a while. I just hope we're pulling into a small town. We need to stock up, so get ready."

The train stopped and Bob quietly slid the door open so he could look out and see what was happening. He pulled back in and said,

"Good news, people are getting out. We must be getting close to Phoenix, but I don't think we're going to stay here very long because some people are getting out but aren't taking any of their suitcases. I'm going to see if I can get us some supplies, but you better stay aboard."

"What if you don't get back in time? What will we do without you?" Caitlyn asked.

"I've never deserted anyone yet, well maybe a couple of scoundrels, but you aren't like them, stay calm and quiet. I'll leave the door open a small bit so you can see out but don't do anything foolish like open it further. Got that?" asked Bob? "Right", they both answered. So, Bob took the bucket to step down on. Then he handed the bucket back and slid the door mostly shut behind him when he reached the ground.

"Now what do we do?" Caitlyn asked.

"Settle down, just be quiet and wait like Bob said," was Billy's reply.

The time dragged by for them as they waited for Bob to return. It seemed a long time but actually was only an hour, before they saw the door start to slide. Billy grabbed Caitlyn, put his finger to his lips, and pulled her over into the corner behind the boxes where the potty pot lived. They heard the door stop and then some grunting as Bob managed to pull himself in.

"It's me kids," he said softly. "You can come out but stay quiet in case someone happens to come by."

They did as he said and signaled him with their hands. He smiled and then held out two big grocery sacks. The kids looked at each other in wonderment at how Bob could buy so much but didn't ask. They smacked their hands against each other's, plus smacked their lips and could hardly wait to eat.

"Let's hear it for Bob," Billy whispered.

Then Bob said, "Stay quiet and let your growling

stomachs make the noise." Caitlyn smiled noiselessly and gave Bob a high five.

The next noise they heard was the engine starting up and they breathed easier knowing no one would be checking the cars. A few minutes later it jerked forward and began moving them along.

"Wow," Billy said to Bob. "Talk about close! You sure cut it close this time. Mr. Bob, is it ok if we open the door again so we see what you brought us?" He asked.

"Wait till I check and make sure we're completely in the clear," replied Bob."

He got up and kind of staggered on his feet over to the door. Caitlyn watched him and whispered to Billy, "Hope he's not had any booze!"

"No, that just comes with old age," Billy whispered back.

Bob must have felt it too because after reaching the door he went back down on his knees. Then slid the door open, peeked out both ways and then slid it further. The sunlight poured in.

"Come on, gather around, I'm inviting you to dinner," Bob said. They did, forming a circle. Then he reached behind his back and pulled out a bag like a magician producing a wonderful display of food. Bob had bought cans of tuna fish, spam, pork and beans, a package of bologna, a head of lettuce, and a big bag of potato chips.

"Wow, Major Bob, you are an awesome performer!" Billy exclaimed.

"Maybe we should call him, the great provider." added Caitlyn.

"I'm impressed, you're both in complete agreement about something. That doesn't happen very often", he added. He reached back behind himself and brought out another bag saying, "I almost forgot this other bag."

"Hope its dessert," Billy said looking at Caitlyn with hopeful anticipation.

"There's bread and yes, Billy, I've got dessert," Bob said, then produced a small cantaloupe.

"Boy, does that stuff look good. I hope you haven't lost your pocketknife and can opener," Caitlyn said.

"No sweetie, I have everything we need, even napkins for our plates. But you know something kids, I have come up with a new idea. From now on each one of us carries our own plates, glasses and silverware. I'm getting tired of doing it all, for all of us, agreed?"

"Yes Sir," Billy snapped and then reaffirmed his promise with a salute.

Caitlyn put a hand over her heart, proclaiming, "I love you from the bottom of my heart," and affirming her agreement to help do her part, she then threw him a kiss.

"Ok kids! Let me make your sandwiches, we need to eat up the bologna now because it won't be any good tomorrow. I'm going to open this can of beans and cut a chunk of lettuce for each of us." They handed him their plates as he took out his pocketknife and can opener to open the beans. It didn't take long for him to load their plates with thick bologna sandwiches, lettuce, beans and chips. When their plates came back to them, the food looked so good they could hardly wait to get started.

"I'll say grace today, I'm afraid you'll both skip over it too fast," Bob said.

They both nodded their head yes and kept them bowed as he proceeded with it in a pretty fast manner because frankly, he was starving just like the young'uns.

"After you finish, pass your plates back so I can give you some melon slices," Bob told them.

They pigged out so much that dinner put them all to sleep.

Chapter Twelve

*E*arly the next morning Bob woke them up with, "The train is slowing down, and I think we're coming into San Diego, our final destination."

"What do you mean, final destination, aren't we going to San Francisco?" asked Billy.

"You're awful forgetful, the way you forget things reminds me of my old granny! Bob already told us we'd have to find another train to get to San Francisco. Duh!" Caitlyn said, shaking her head.

Then mischievously she added, "The first thing I'd like to find is a bakery where I can get something sweet. Being around you guys so long gives me that craving."

"Thanks, you're a real sweetheart too!" retaliated Billy.

"Ok kids! Stop that bickering, it isn't a good way to start the day. It'd be better to thank God that we all found each other and are still healthy and alive after such a trip," said the peace maker.

"You're right, Bob, and I'm sure grateful to be under your care. Did you ever have any kids of your own?" Caitlyn asked.

"No, I'm sorry to say that wasn't in the cards for me. I never met any woman I wanted to share my life with. The closest I ever came was a woman called Mary. That relationship lasted about six months which was a long time for me since I've always been the wandering type and never really content to stay long in any one place. But, hey, God must have felt sorry for me because He brought you two to me and put you in my heart."

Bob smiled and reached out for a hug. Both of them crawled over into his embrace. It was a special moment.

"Well, Bob, guess you got lucky in your cards this time, us too," laughed Billy.

"Thank you very much, young man."

Billy laughed again, "You sound like that singer, Elvis. Uh, what's his last name?"

Bob didn't answer, just told them to gather up all their stuff because this ride had stopped.

"Hold on, let me slide the door open to check outside and see if this is the right time for us to check out of our hotel room." Bob finally said.

He went over to the door then quietly slid it open so he could see what was going on.

Then he said, "I think it's a good time. There's a lot of commotion with people getting off with suitcases so let's get going too."

He slid the door open, turned around, picked up his bag and jumped out. The two kids looked at each other in surprise because he landed great on his own two feet without any help.

"Wow, I never saw him do that before. You know

I always went first with the bucket so he could climb out and down using it as his personal ladder," said an astonished Billy.

"Maybe that was how he thought he would take back his dignity", Caitlyn surmised, who quickly jumped out too. Billy followed her out and whether or not he meant it as a joke, she didn't know, but he landed on his feet too, and then fell over. Happily, they went into the station walking through the crowd and out the front entrance.

There were a lot of people standing out there waiting and waving to the arriving passengers. Bob said to the young'uns,

"Smile and wave at someone so we look like all the rest of the passengers. Then we'll work our way through the crowd without notice, just in case there's a railroad inspector among them watching for people like us."

They did and breathed a sigh of relief as they reached the sidewalk without anyone stopping them. They went down the street for a couple of blocks and Bob stopped in front of a hotel.

"What are you stopping for?" Billy inquired.

"Well, kids! I have a surprise. You're going to be my guest tonight!"

It didn't take Bob long to get registered and return for the kids. They were both happy at the surprise because this was another new experience.

"Gather up your stuff and follow me" he said, "and don't say anything."

They did, but when they got inside the reception area, both of them stopped.

"What's the matter?" Bob asked.

"It's so big and pretty in here", answered Caitlyn. "I've never seen anything like this before."

"Yeah, you're not exaggerating, it's great! I can't wait to see our room," cried Billy.

"But, Bob, how many beds are in the room? I don't want to sleep on the floor, but a couch would be ok. The one thing I don't want to do is sleep with her!" Billy said.

"Ditto," she said. "Nor do I with him."

"Come on, let's get on that elevator over there in the corner. We'll settle this matter when we get to our room," Bob told them.

"What floor, Sir?" asked the elevator operator.

"Fifth floor, please," Bob told him.

"Wow, fifth floor, I hope it's got a lot of windows so I can see out over the city, or at least part of it." Billy commented.

"I just hope our room is facing the front of the building, not the ones on the side. Or worse, the back of the building and have just an alley to look at. But anything will be better than that dark, noisy train we've been riding," added Caitlyn softly.

The elevator stopped, Bob thanked the man as the door opened and he stood aside so they could get out.

Bob said, "Wish I'd thought to ask him which direction our room number is. I guess we can go one direction then the other, if necessary, to find it. Come on let's look to the right."

They both agreed and then Billy asked,

"What's the number?"

Bob looked at the key and said, "Fifty-five."

"Hope that's your lucky number Mr. Bob!"

Bob laughed and started walking down the hall. He came to a dead end and then turned left. That hallway dead ended at a window which looked out to the front of the hotel. Bob looked to the right and there was their room. He unlocked the door and they went in happily to find it had not one, but two windows to look out of.

"We got lucky on the windows", stated Billy, "But I only see two small beds in here."

Billy seemed overly concerned about the number of beds and knew there was no way he was going to share a bed with Caitlyn. And on such a narrow bed he knew Bob would be all over him if he shared his. Bob sensed his concern.

"They're called twin beds and I've requested a cot be brought in for a third bed."

"Who gets the cot, whatever that is?" Billy asked still not satisfied with Bob's answer.

"You'll just have to trust me on this, or maybe we can flip a coin for the bed. Who wants heads?"

"Caitlyn, ladies first, what do you say, heads or tails?"

"Heads," she answered.

Bob reached into his pocket, pulled out a nickel, flipped it and lady luck was with Caitlyn.

"Yes, thank you!" she yelled.

"Ok, now that we've settled that, let's go get something to eat. The extra bed won't be brought in for a while. I'll let them know at the front desk we are going out. So out we go!" and headed them toward the door.

They followed him out to the elevator and then they stopped at the front desk where he had ordered the extra cot. With that done, out the door they went to stop and look in both directions.

"What kind of dinner do you want?" asked Bob.

"I'd love some fried chicken and apple pie", declared Billy.

"What about you, Caitlyn?" Bob asked.

"Well Sir, I don't really care. I'd just like to eat a good meal, hopefully one not too costly," she responded.

"I'm just going to be enjoying the sights of this big town or city, whatever it's called."

"I think it's still San Diego. What do you think Billy?" Bob asked.

Billy wasn't sure either. "Why don't we go to the right?" he added. "Maybe that's the direction Ole' Fate is showing us. Get it? Right is the 'right' direction."

"Really Billy? What do you know about Fate?" Then Caitlyn said, "Let's flip for it." She was still feeling lucky. And just because Billy wanted to go right, she said, "I chose tails to go left."

"Good idea," said Bob, and dug into his pants pocket, drew out a nickel and flipped it. Heads it was.

Gleefully, Billy smacked her on the shoulder and said, "So there."

"Ok, let's get started, before the restaurants all close down for the night and Billy starves to death," Bob said and started walking with his sheep following. Several blocks down the street he stopped at a place called 'Granny's Kitchen' and asked them what they thought of this one.

Caitlyn said, "It looks good to me, probably lots of home cooked choices. What do you two, think?" They nodded their heads yes, and went in.

They were greeted at the front door by a lady wearing a white apron. Billy thought she looked like the cook, not a waitress, but he was wrong because she said,

"Please follow me and I will take you to a table."

When seated she handed them a menu and said, "Take your time and decide what you want, I'll be back in a few minutes."

Bob thought to himself, "She wants us to take our time, then says she'll be back in a few minutes! Maybe this is just 'west coast' thinking?"

She returned directly and asked for their orders.

It didn't take Billy long to order. "I want the fried chicken, mashed potatoes with gravy, green beans, and of course apple pie. No! I want cherry pie this time with vanilla ice cream on it."

"That sounds good to me too," Caitlyn agreed.

"Make that a threesome Miss, if you would," requested Bob.

"Billy, isn't it your turn to say grace?" Bob asked.

"Regardless of whose turn it is, shouldn't we wait for the food?" Billy asked.

They all felt relieved to finally be some place and laughed too loud to suit the lady seated at the next table because she said to her partner;

"Wonder where these ill-mannered and noisy people came from? The hills?"

Then her companion said, "Please, Sarah, don't be rude!"

The lady put her napkin to her mouth, then excused herself from the table and walked away. The man with her watched her, wondering where she was going. Probably, she was going to the Ladies room, to the front desk to complain to the one in charge, or just walking out the front door. He hoped it was the third one as this was their first date and he prayed, "Please God, make it the last!" It was because she huffed her way out the front door.

Bob and his noisy dinner partners watched her go out. Then Bob said to the guy left at his table;

"I'm sorry if we ruined your evening."

Billy and Caitlyn said, "We are sorry too."

The guy said, "Actually, you all did me a favor. I didn't know her very well and don't want to, after seeing how she acted. Thank you for helping me out. By the way, the food here is great and now I'm ready to eat, excuse me." Eagerly he dug into his food with relish.

No more conversation was necessary as their waitress arrived with their food. Bob thought, "Her timing was perfect, or maybe it's God's. I'm going to give Him thanks right now and did."

Bob smiled at Caitlyn who followed his eyes

directed at Billy. He couldn't wait any longer for the taste of fried chicken and had already bit into a chicken leg. There was silence then, except for the smacking of lips and silverware clicking.

Of course, the first one done with the main course was Billy and asked Bob, "Will the waitress be coming around soon with my desert?"

"I don't know but it would be polite if you could be patient and wait for Caitlyn and me to finish our chicken before you start with your pie. What do you think, can you wait?" he asked.

"Yeah, that would be kind of nice," Caitlyn added.

"I'm sorry," Billy said a little embarrassed.

"Apology accepted and now missy, let's do our best not to make him wait much longer, ok?"

In not more than five minutes the other two did a quick job of finishing up just before the waitress arrived with dessert. In spite of the hefty meal of fried chicken with mashed potatoes and gravy, it didn't take long for them to finish the pie and ice cream.

Bob picked up the bill she'd also left with the desert, studied it, and then reached in his rear pocket and pulled out his billfold. He took out a couple of dollars and laid them on the table.

"Ok, kids! Let's go up to the front desk so I can pay this bill."

Outside Billy patted his belly,

"Thank you, Bob! That was probably the best meal I ever had!"

"Me, too," Caitlyn joined in, patting her belly like

Billy though being more feminine about it. She didn't realize it yet, but on this trip, she had become a young lady.

"I'd pat my belly, too," Bob said. "But I don't want to call attention to how big it's getting. What's interesting is how it's managed to do that with me riding the rails." He laughed a little but said, "All this food has made me sleepy so maybe we should all head back to our hotel room."

"Bob, I'm not ready for a nap, so could Caitlyn and I look at the stores along the street?"

"Yes, please," added Caitlyn.

"All right but stay on the same street and do not talk to anyone, Bob ordered. I'll meet you back outside in two hours, at least that's my plan. If I'm not outside by then come in and wake me up, got it?"

"Yes, Sir," they promised simultaneously, giving him their salutes.

Billy and Caitlyn walked down the street for a while looking into the store windows. Then Caitlyn stopped, sat down on a bench and looking up at Billy patting the space beside her. He lowered himself down by her and asked;

"Why are we stopping, we really don't have a lot of time to see many more places?"

"I have a request. I had a real nice grandma but only had a short time to know her. She died when I was just starting second grade. Something I'd like you to do is to call me by my nickname like she used to do. She said Caitlyn seemed too formal for her and called me,

'Katie'. You are my best friend ever, so I'd like for you to call me Katie, like my Grandma did."

"Well thanks," Billy said feeling a little embarrassed talking to a girl like this for the first time. "You are the best friend I ever had too, but what about Bob?"

"I wasn't thinking about grownups," Katie answered.

"Ok, that makes sense, so what should I call you and is it to be only when we're by ourselves?" Billy asked.

"No, I guess we can tell Bob and then he can make his own choice, but will you call me Katie?"

"Sure, I'll call you Katie." Billy's face felt a little red and was anxious to be on their way. He said, "But we've still got some time left before Bob gets up, about an hour."

They both got up and wandered along the street. They saw a lot of stuff they'd like to have, but unfortunately couldn't afford anything except for the bakery where they each bought a donut. The time seemed to fly by, and they felt their time must be up. When they stopped a woman wearing a wristwatch, she told them the time and they knew for sure, they were running a little late, like fifteen minutes.

"Catch me if you can!" Billy shouted and took off running down the sidewalk toward the hotel.

Bob was standing out in front and when they reached him. He looked at his watch and then at them, "Running a bit late, aren't you?"

Billy replied, "Sorry sir, we didn't have a watch."

"Ditto," she said. "I'm sorry too. I hope you aren't upset at us."

"Well, I'll have to think about it. But for now, let's go strolling," he frowned at each of them as if he was thinking and then he turned left. They looked at each other but started following, maybe not quite as close as before.

They walked several blocks to an area Bob said was the square and started around it.

"Wow! Katie and I didn't go in this direction, this place is pretty neat. Do you want to sit a while and rest on one of these benches?" Billy suggested.

"Sounds like a good idea, I'm not as young as I used to be or like you two are now." Then he looked at the girl, and said, "Katie?"

She answered, "It's my nickname. You may call me that if you'd like to."

They all sat together and stared at the fountain in front of them. Then Billy got up to have a closer look. He stared for a couple of minutes then came back to the others.

"Bob, people around here must be rich because there's a lot of coins in the bottom of that fountain! Bet there's some poor folks cleaning it out in the night."

"I want to have a closer look too, do you Bob?" Caitlyn asked.

"No, you kids go on over, I'm just going to rest here and watch the town folks stroll by. By the way, people make a wish and then throw the money in. You two want to make a wish? If you do, here's three nickels for us. Use one and make a wish for me too, ok?"

"What do you want to wish for?" asked Billy.

"Well, let me see. Tell you what, I'll let you know later. For now, just say this for my wish and pitch my nickel in. I'm sure the good fairy, or whoever is in charge, will honor my wish," he nodded his head and waved them on.

They went back over to him and Caitlyn asked, "Billy, what are you going to wish for?"

"I don't have the least idea what I want except maybe for this adventure to never end."

"And I wish we would end up in the gold fields where we could get rich!" he said excitedly.

"You go first, Billy, because I have to ponder what my request will be. Hey though, wonder if we could make more than one wish? I still got a little money left in my pocket, do you?" She asked.

"Yeah, but I don't want to be selfish or greedy. If my one wish comes true that's enough."

"I guess that makes sense so I'm only going to do one wish like you," she agreed.

They both did theirs and Bob's wish, then went back over to him. He was standing up waiting for them. "Done?" he inquired.

They said "Yes," and then Bob said, "Ok, let's get started back. As we were walking here, I saw a small grocery store across the street that had some fruits and stuff setting out front. I want to buy our dinner there. It'll be cheaper than going to another restaurant. We can eat in our room but be careful not to let the hotel management see us take food upstairs. I don't think they would allow food in the rooms. We can have the store person put it in three small bags, so the hotel people probably won't notice."

They went in and Bob choose some buns, baloney, potato chips, pears, cookies, and pop. He paid for them and instructed the clerk to put them in three bags. He did but couldn't help wondering why Bob wanted three bags and not just one big bag. But, he did what he was asked to do.

They reached the hotel confidently carrying their bags into the lobby, over to the elevator and into their room.

"Good job, kids! Now let's wash up and get started on dinner. Hand me those pears so I can wash them up." Bob said. They joined together on the floor to eat but first saying grace. He told them to join hands and asked Billy and then Katie to also say grace as it had been a special day for all of them. It was a special day! They had all enjoyed being together.

Bob turned the television set on, and they watched it until they were ready for bed. When it was turned off Bob said;

"Get a good night's rest because I have something very special to tell you both in the morning."

Chapter Thirteen

Bob was the first one awake so after using the bathroom he returned to wake up his young roommates. His face was shaved clean for the first time in so long he hardly recognized himself. He wondered what the young'uns would think of him. Since Billy was up a tad bit sooner than Caitlyn, he made it to the bathroom first. He smirked at her and Bob just shook his head.

"We all need a bath this morning before we leave our room," Bob reminded the others.

When Billy looked at Bob nothing was said, and Bob raised an eyebrow in surprise. But when Caitlyn came out and saw him, she gave a gasp of surprise thinking a stranger was in their room.

"It's me," he assured her. "Don't run."

After they were all cleaned up, they left their room and went into the hotel's dining room to eat breakfast. A hearty breakfast of bacon, eggs, toast and jelly tasted so good. Bob wanted coffee with his breakfast, but Billy and Katie preferred orange juice. Whether it was because of hunger or just the habit of eating whatever they had, no one cared.

After they finished eating, Bob told them about a park not too far away that he wanted them to see and Billy remembered what Bob had said the night before.

"Last night you said you had something special to tell us, what about that?"

"I'm coming to that," Bob answered. He patted Billy on the shoulder. "The park will be a perfect place to tell you."

Since Bob said the park was nearby, they set out walking and as he said, it wasn't very far away. It was a beautiful part of the city and crowds of people enjoyed it all year round. Caitlyn and Billy marveled at the different kinds of greenery, animals and people. That alone made it a special day but still they couldn't help being curious. Billy hoped it would be traveling news. He was ready to go find some gold. Caitlyn was at peace because for the first time in her life she felt loved and cared for. Whatever the future had in store for her, she was content to go anywhere with her two new friends.

Bob led them to a pond, and they sat down beside it on the ground. The kids took off their shoes and put their feet in the water. It was cool and soothing to their tired feet.

"Hey Bob, aren't you going to cool your feet? It feels great!" Caitlyn asked.

"Sorry kids, but I washed my feet this morning when I took my bath," he stated with a wink.

Caitlin said, "That's funny, but didn't you ever say, 'don't look a gift horse in the mouth,' of course this isn't exactly a horse, right Billy?"

"Oh brother," Billy moaned. "I mean sister, but yes, I agree."

"The first matter of business Bob said, is to say I'm sorry Billy, but we're not going to San Francisco for two reasons. The first one is that the gold rush there happened around a hundred years ago and I doubt very much if there's any left. The second reason is my uncle that used to live here died a couple of years ago. And since I am his oldest living relative, he left everything to me. It's a big farm close by and I've had some of his money for over a year. I decided to come back from New York, riding my last journey on a train like I had done for so many years. My cash didn't come from gambling, Billy. Sorry, I let you think so, but I thought it would be smarter not to let anyone know I was carrying a bundle of cash. To be safe, I had to make both of you think gambling money was all I had."

"I can't believe you've been lying to us all this time. I don't know what to think. But I guess I'm kinda used to grownups lying to me." Billy mumbled.

"Hey buddy, don't be so judgmental, he's been real good to us, keeping us safe from all kinds of dangerous people, and from starving." Katie added.

"You're right Katie. Sorry Bob, but I hope the second reason doesn't mean you're leaving us to fend for ourselves. I'd understand if you do though," he said looking out over the water. He could hardly look Bob in the eye for fear he was right.

"No Billy, I'm not leaving you, and I really do want

the legal right to call you my son so I'm hiring a lawyer to make this happen; for you too Katie, so I can call you my daughter!"

Billy and Katie both could have been knocked over with a feather, they stood motionless with mouths agape, letting the meaning of Bob's words sink in.

"Well, that shouldn't be too hard in my case, but what do you think, Katie?" asked Billy.

"My mean ole' stepdad will probably try to get money out of you," she replied.

"That's ok, honey! My lawyer has a lot of smarts and knows how to make things like this work. I don't want you to worry one minute, just trust in the good Lord. Yes, I know, Billy, it sounds like I'm getting religious, doesn't it? But I was raised in the Catholic Church and it's time I got back to it. I will expect you two to also go with me every Sunday. Do you agree with that?"

Billy said, "I don't mind church, but I'd prefer to go to a regular school and not a Catholic one. What about you, Katie?"

"I couldn't care less about the school. But it's the teachers and kids that are the ones important to me. Most of the kids I knew at school poked fun at me and the clothes I had to wear," Katie shared.

"Well sweetheart, you won't be in that position again because I won't tolerate anyone, teachers included, making you feel bad. This world is hard sometimes, but we can sure ask the Good Lord to help us when we are in trouble" replied Bob.

"Hey, better be careful Bob, or Dad, you're starting

to sound like a preacher," Billy laughed. "I promise to make you a good son."

"Ok but you've got to be patient with me because this role of dad is completely new to me. Like I've told you, I've never even been married let alone be a father," he added.

"Now let's go get us a taxi and head out to our new home."

Bob was like a savior to Billy and Katie and with the help of the real Savior, managed to turn their life around. The adoptions went through and thus began a new chapter in all their lives.

Dedicated to my daughter Michele:

Michele

'A New Life'

Chapter One

Indiana

"I'm leaving you Doris. I've found someone else. Her name is Ella. Not only does she have some money, but she also has time to appreciate my company," Harry announced.

The Great Depression of 1929 had settled in across the country making it hard for most folks to have any real money. Harry and Doris were no exception and with Harry's health problems, life was harder for them than it should have been.

It was 1932 and Michele was just four years old when she heard her dad say those words to her mom. They remain as her only memory of him. He was a selfish, self-centered man and since Doris was busy with their new baby Jane, just six months old. She expected Harry to help with the four older children, but he didn't want any part of helping with the kids.

Michele was four years old, Dave seven, Bob ten and Jenny twelve. "They're old enough to take care of themselves," He declared.

She couldn't give him the wifely attention he

thought he should have, and it was then she knew how self-centered he was, since he deserted them.

A divorce followed, but unfortunately Doris only held contempt for Harry. She was bitter! In the courtroom, she told the judge,

"I don't want anything from Harry but a place to raise my kids, just let him go," she declared.

The judge must have been irritated with him as well because even though Harry didn't make much as a carpenter due to his hypochondriac condition, the judge said to her;

"Ma'am, you might not want anything right now, but you will later. I'm ordering him to pay you five dollars a week child support."

That didn't help very much but their marriage was over. She didn't know how, but Doris left the courtroom with their kids determined to earn enough to raise them herself. The years to follow were hard for her but she didn't give up. Her eleventh-grade education didn't help her find anything but hard work.

She rented an upstairs two-bedroom apartment in the center of Ada, Ohio and found work as a maid at a hotel just four buildings from their apartment. She added to her meager salary by taking in people's clothes to wash, and she ironed the ones that required ironing.

The kitchen sink had the only drain for her wringer washing machine, so after running the clothes through the wringer, she put them in a basket. Then she emptied the wash water out into a bucket to pour down the kitchen sink. Next, she filled the tank again with clean cold water for the clothes to go back into. The machine was plugged back in and turned on to get rid of the soap. Everything had to be run through the wringer again into the rinse water.

Her clothes lines were outside on the rooftop of the bar below. They were shaped like a cross with all the support poles in large buckets filled with cement. If it was raining or cold, she hung two ropes from wall to wall in the kitchen. The four kitchen table chairs were also used as clothes racks.

One day a wise looking, middle aged man came home with her. She introduced him to the kids as George. Jenny and Bob looked at each other and Bob finally asked,

"Is he going to be our new dad?"

"Goodness no!" Doris said, shocked as much as the kids were at the very idea.

"George is going to be a boarder with us, that's all. He will sleep on a cot."

"What's a boarder, Mommy?" Michele asked.

"A boarder means he will pay us money to sleep here and eat if he wants to, that's all."

They were all relieved, especially Bob, to hear George would be just a boarder and nothing more. After the way their dad had left, he didn't want another man taking his place.

Since Doris didn't have a dining room table, George's cot occupied the space between the kitchen and living room. She provided him oatmeal for breakfast and a supper meal with them for five dollars a week. George boarded with them the next two years.

He worked at the Ada Daily News, a local newspaper, located one block down the alley from where they lived. The building had windows overlooking the alley on one of its sides that could be opened for fresh air. When Michele felt the call to be creative, she used chalk to draw on the building opposite the Ada Daily News. One afternoon she was quite startled when a man called through one of the opened windows at her.

"Young lady, what are you doing?"

"None of your darn business!" Michele yelled back at him and took off back down the alley to their apartment.

Later that day, before her mom got home, the renter informed her that he was the one who saw her marking on the building and had yelled at her. She hung her head then, embarrassed at what she had said to him.

"I'm sorry", she said, "please don't tell my mom."

"Ok, if you promise never to write or draw on buildings again, and don't use bad words!"

"Yes, I swear!" she replied.

"No, no don't swear," he laughingly demanded.

"But that's what the cowboys say when they promise to do or not do something," she replied.

George, overhearing, looked around as if looking for something and then asked,

"Don't you have any paper to draw on?"

"Well, there is the paper the grocer uses to wrap meat in. Of course, I have to let it dry out and then cover up the bloody spots with my crayons. Then I use my pen and pencil to draw with."

She admitted, "Sometimes I help myself to the teacher's typing paper too."

"Kid, you're a piece of work!", George replied.

She knew they needed his rent money, so she hoped he was convinced but to be sure, she said,

"I'm sorry Sir. I promise not to steal paper from school or anywhere else, ok?"

"Well," George replied. "We'll see what you do in the future."

The future wasn't too kind to Michele but there was one good thing that came out of her rebellion. One day, she and her brother Dave were staring out of one of the two front windows overlooking Main Street. Half a block away was the center of town where events were held in an open area. Someone had built a six-sided podium about five feet tall with steps leading from the cement covered ground up to the top of the platform, where the speaker or a music conductor would stand.

Michele and Dave were so intrigued by the sight of the podium that when he said; "Let's go down there and see it better," she didn't hesitate.

"Ok brother, let's do it!"

When they got there, no one else was around so Dave said, "Come on, let's climb up the steps."

Again, she agreed, "Ok," and climbed the steps behind Dave up to the platform. As usual whatever Dave wanted to do, they did.

But when Dave decided to look over the banister, he leaned out way too far, lost his balance and fell onto the cement below.

Michele climbed down the stairs and ran over to where Dave sat with his right hand on his forehead. When he brought it down, she saw blood coming from a cut over his eye.

"Your face is bleeding!" She screamed.

He got up and headed to the alley behind their apartment building. Michele ran after him wondering why he went down the alley, the long way around, instead of going back across to the front entrance. After running up the back stairs and through the kitchen door, she huffed out,

"Why did we come home the longer way?"

"Because more people could see me if we stayed on Main Street!" he said.

Luckily, a few minutes later their mom came in the back door. She was shocked to see blood on Dave's face and immediately took him into the bathroom. She washed the blood away, examined the cut and realizing it was going to need stitches.

"Michele, stay here, I've got to take him to see Dr. Brown!"

She rushed Dave to the doctor's office and Michele waited for what seemed hours until they finally returned. Dave had a bandage that wrapped completely around his head. He looked whipped.

"Go to your bedroom and lie down," Doris told him.

Then turning to Michele, she said, "You know what's next, go get the paddle!"

Michele was frightened when her mom looked like this but handed it over to her as she was sitting on a kitchen chair.

"Lay down across my lap!" she said.

"Dave has already received his punishment and now you are going to get yours."

She began spanking the confused girl who couldn't help thinking how unfair this was because it was Dave's idea for them to go over to the square, not hers; she had just followed him. Because of this, Michele decided she wouldn't give her mom the satisfaction of seeing or hearing her cry and held the tears back.

When Doris stopped and let her get up, the rebellious kid said,

"Is that all you got?", which got her a slap in the face!

The good part of that day was that she never received another slap or spanking. She was basically a good kid who would try to help and please others, but only if they asked her, and didn't try to force her into it.

Chapter Two

Dave's attraction to trouble was like a magnet to metal. It was like trouble called to him. For example, Doris told them to stay away from the Wages River which flowed through Ada. And they were especially forbidden to go anywhere near it in the wintertime. Occasionally, during the summertime Bob went fishing there with a pole he found and with the meat wrapper's string on the end for a line. He could find all the night crawlers he wanted for bait. They were out at night especially following a rain. Then, if he got lucky there was a nearby restaurant owner who would buy his fish. This gave him a bit of spending money for anything that was made of chocolate.

Dave and his buddy, Rick, would hang out there lots of the times, not doing anything profitable, just skipping stones across the water. They loved it when it was covered with ice. In spite of Doris's specific warning not to go near the river during cold weather, they slid on it like they wore ice skates.

One day Bob went looking for them and found the silly boys had slid across the river to the other side.

"Get over here where you belong!" he yelled.

"Go home brother! I don't need you. Go find our sisters and boss them around if you don't have anything better to do," Dave shouted back to them.

Evidently, he didn't, as he started walking on the ice toward them. He reached the other side and pushed them ahead of him back toward the side where they belonged. They were about four feet from the shore when the ice started cracking. Dave and Rick made it safely to land, but Bill didn't and fell through the ice. He could touch bottom so with a big lunge, he grabbed a hold of Dave's outstretched hand and crawled to safety. His only injury was a scrape on his chin but otherwise he was not hurt.

When Doris got home that night and saw his face, she wanted to know how it happened.

"Were you in fight, or what?"

Bob ratted Dave out and that was the straw that broke the camel's back.

Doris said to them, "I've had enough of this kind of behavior, I'm sorry boys but I can't take care of you anymore. It doesn't matter what I tell you not to do, you always wind up doing it anyway. My efforts to raise you right haven't been enough, I'm going to call your dad."

After the phone call, Ella took on more responsibility, Bob and Dave. It worked out good for Harry. He taught them his trade of carpentry, and he didn't have to pay them as he would have other workers. Ella also raised a big garden plus had her salary from a job at the local underwear factory. With a regular salary, she could buy any other groceries she needed to feed them.

Old Harry didn't try to get his child support lowered either. Guess he was afraid a different judge might even raise it.

The boy's new home was in Mayville, about five miles east of Ada. There was just a short distance separating them, but the two younger sisters only saw them at Christmas time for a couple of days and two weeks during the summer.

Michele was devastated when Bob and Dave were sent away; first her dad and now her brothers. Bob was there only a short time when one night he confided to his brother that he was running away on a train and did.

"Who's next?" Michele wondered, hoping her mother wasn't the one, because Jenny wasn't available to fill her place. Michele didn't want her and Jane ending up in the children's home, but then again, she had no idea what that would be like. But that would mean giving up her new job in the bar below their apartment that none of her family knew about.

Strangely enough the bar had an ice cream cooler that sat at one end of the bar. And Jack, the bartender would fill a cone with one or two scoops of vanilla, chocolate or strawberry. One scoop was five cents and two scoops cost a dime. An ice cream cone was mainly what Michele worked for.

Jack was a pretty lenient bartender to let a seven-year-old girl dance on top of the bar but figured the live entertainment would help the slow business pick up during the daytime. Mainly, all that came to the bar during the day were four old regulars.

One of them, Howard, could have had her fired from her dancing job if he had pushed the matter. One day Jack raised her up onto the bar to do her dance and asked her if she wanted something fast or slow. She chose "My Love" sung by Nat King Cole. After her decision, he went over and put money in the juke box. Then as usual at the end of her dance, she went down the bar to collect her tips.

This time Howard pulled a trick on her. Michele was to learn a lesson about the ways of the world. The first three men put some change on the bar for Michele to pick up, but Howard didn't put anything out as the other men down the line had.

She looked down at him boldly and said,

"What's wrong, didn't you like my dance?"

He looked up at her and replied,

"I guess it was ok," then reached into his pants pocket and pulled out a penny, laid it on the bar and then shoved it over to her.

"Just ok, huh? Well, thanks a lot!" Michele reached down, picked up his penny and dropped it in his glass of whiskey. Smiling to herself she jumped down off the bar and went out the back door with her money instead of buying an ice cream cone.

"I wish I knew where that ole' man lives", she thought, "and I'd put a token of appreciation on his front door. There's plenty of cow manure at that cow slaughtering factory over by the bridge."

The next week she was a little afraid she'd lost her job but evidently Jack was a forgiving boss because when she came in, he said, "Hi Michele! Ready to dance?" and lifted her up onto the bar? Ole' Howard must have been forgiving too, because he actually put a dime tip out for her after she finished her dance.

Chapter Three

*T*hat summer Michele found another way to earn some money that was totally unexpected. She was so skinny her classmates said her legs looked like toothpicks and she was always scared Ole' Howard would say something about them especially since she ruined his drink, but he didn't. She couldn't help wondering if his drinking buddies, who always tipped her, might have felt sorry for her and gave her a little extra tip.

Evidently that summer, Doris decided she was too thin and took Michele to see a doctor at the outskirts of Ada. She told him how Michele seemed to have a good appetite but was still too thin and didn't know what to do.

"Maybe she eats so much, it makes her poor to carry it," he said jokingly. Doris didn't laugh at his joke, but Michele did laugh out of embarrassment.

The doctor added, "I'm sorry Ma'am, I was just kidding. As you saw, I've checked her over and didn't find anything wrong, so please don't worry. I have something I want you to try that may help her gain some weight. It's a tonic a drug-salesmen gave me samples of, and I'll give you a bottle to try. Just follow the directions on the bottle and let me know what you think. If it works for her, I'll give you more of it."

Doris replied, "Thank you doctor, I surely will." She was grateful the doctor had given her the tonic at no cost and hoped it would help Michele.

They went home and the next morning before she left for work Doris mixed up a pint canning jar with the tonic powder and milk. She handed it to Michele who looked at the chocolaty colored mix, anxious to taste it but still uncertain. She should have taken a small sip to taste but instead took a big mouthful. The chocolate color had fooled her. It tasted awful! She swallowed, then coughed to clear her mouth of the taste and cried out, "This is terrible, Mom!"

Doris responded, "I don't care if it does taste terrible. It was free, but it still cost me five dollars to see the doctor. Do you realize that's one whole week's child support I get from your dad?"

"I'm sorry Mom," was all Michele could think of to say.

"Since you're on summer vacation you've got all day to be home," Doris explained, "but I don't! I'm running late for work. But let me tell you Michele, when I get home tonight this jar better be empty and you better not have thrown it away either. Do you hear me?" She asked Michele the question as if she was in the next room instead of facing her.

"Yes Mom, I hear you and I promise I won't throw it away." Michele answered.

"Well, you better not, I'll see you tonight. And behave yourself. Don't take your unhappiness out on your sisters either." Before going out the kitchen door she looked at Michele one last time and said, "Behave yourself today," as if she didn't always behave.

Michele felt miserable. There was no way she could stand to drink the whole jar full. Even a small swallow of that chocolaty mixture made her gag. She carried it outside and at the bottom of the stairs looked across the alley at the roofers who were gathered talking and preparing for their day's work.

They always talked nice to Michele and since she was in need of some encouragement, she walked over to them.

"Hey, kid, what's in that jar?" One of the men asked.

She felt embarrassed to be truthful but then an idea sprang up in her mind.

"It's just a drink my mom fixes for me."

"Is it good?" he asked.

"Oh yeah, do you want to try it?" She enticed him into trying it by passing the jar over to him.

"Sure," he said, and took a drink.

"This isn't too bad. You guys want to try it?" He asked the other men then passed it to the next guy who took a drink.

"Yeah, this is pretty good. Here buddy, want to try it." And by the time they had all taken a drink of the chocolaty colored mix the whole jar was empty.

"Oh, my goodness guys, look what we did!"

"Here kid," one said as he reached into his pants

pocket for some money. Evidently a dime was all the change he had. Then he said, "Ok men, let's all pitch in a dime to pay for her drink."

They wound up giving Michele five dimes. Both surprised at the money and grateful her drink was all gone, she thanked them and said, "If you want, I'll bring you another one tomorrow, ok?"

"Yes, sounds like a plan, ok with you guys?"

"Sure, sure, sure, sure," each of them agreed.

That night when Doris returned home, Michele met her in the kitchen.

"Hey Mom, guess what? That drink turned out to be a good idea. Here's the empty jar. I didn't rinse it out so you could see it. I don't know why I acted like I did when I first tasted it, unless it was because of that stick of licorice I had just eaten before I tasted the tonic. It wasn't so bad after all. I'm fine with it now Mom, thanks."

"You are a sweet girl," she said approvingly.

"Ok, young lady, just remember not to eat any candy or even chew any bubble gum before you drink it. In fact, drink it before you eat anything. Do I make myself clear?" Her mom asked.

"Yes, Mother, you do."

"Did you just call me, Mother?" Doris asked her.

"Well this is a special occasion and I want to respect your wishes. Sometimes I forget, but you deserve it all the time. I can only imagine how hard it is to raise us girls all by yourself." Michele retorted.

"I hope you never have to Michele. Come here so I can give you a hug," Her mom replied.

Since Doris wasn't an emotional person, it was a surprise to her daughter who was seldom hugged by her mother. She also felt a bit of guilt knowing the lie she told her mother earned her this loving touch. She knew it was a hard world out there, and her mother could never give up. Michele could only fight for her place in life, which she did two weeks later.

Michele took the drink out to the men for the next ten days. Then one morning, she slept later than usual and unfortunately didn't get her drink out to the roofers as usual. Her sister Jenny was up early though, to go help their elderly grandmother, Nora, spring clean her house. She was making a short cut through the back alley and one of the roofers stopped her to ask if Michele was alright.

"Yes, why do you want to know?" Jenny inquired.

"Well, she sells us that drink every morning and she hasn't been out today," he replied.

"What drink are you talking about?" Jenny demanded to know.

"Well, get off your high horse and I'll tell you!" he said.

She answered, "Ok, I'm sorry, but she's always causing trouble at home, in school, or wherever she goes. Since I'm the oldest, Mom holds me responsible, as if anyone other than the good Lord could stop her shenanigans!"

He could see Jenny felt frustrated with her sister.

"Ok, well since you're apologizing, I'll tell you. I don't know what the drink is, but it's kind of chocolaty and she brings it in a pint canning jar," he replied.

"That's a tonic the doctor gave Mom for her!" Jenny exclaimed knowing Michele was up to one of her tricks.

"What! Do you mean the doctor wants her to drink this and we have been doing it for her? And she isn't supposed to be selling it to us?" he asked.

"That's exactly right, and when I tell my mother I can assure you she won't be doing it anymore. Just wait until my mother gets home today. She'll be in a heap of trouble." Jenny barked back!

After the indigent older sister declared the truth to the men, she turned around in a huff only to be met by the criminal in question who just happened to hear the threat to her latest enterprise.

"Sis! Wait a minute! I can explain," Michele pleaded.

"Get out of my way I'm late. Some of us have a responsibility but I don't think you even know what that word means!" Jenny said as she stalked away.

"I'm sorry guys I was just trying to earn some money and I guess I blew it," Michele told them.

"It's ok sweetheart. We understand, right fellows?" One of them said to calm Michele.

"But we sure are going to miss that drink every morning. In fact, I felt more like working after you brought us that tonic!" replied her customer.

"Thank you for understanding, I'll see you later," she said and strode off.

The troubled young'un spent the rest of the day trying

to figure out how to settle the problem. Unfortunately, she couldn't. Her sister didn't change her mind either and told their mother as soon as she got home.

Michele hid in her bedroom that evening waiting to hear from her mother, after Jenny told about what she had been doing. Her mother was tired and worn out from a long day's work. It wasn't a good time to hear bad news.

"Come here, you little liar," she called to Michele still hiding in her bedroom.

Michele emerged slowly saying, "I'm sorry Mom. That stuff tasted horrible and you only made me promise not to throw it away!"

"But I didn't tell you to sell it!" her mother declared. "What did you do with the money?"

"Come on outside and I'll get it for you. It's in a tobacco can I hid in the ground under the stairs," she confessed.

Doris followed her out the kitchen door and watched as Michele went down the stairs, picked up a small piece of wood and dug out the treasure. She handed her treasured tin can to her mother to open and to take out the money. To her surprise when she counted it, there was exactly five dollars.

"Well, isn't this something? The same amount I paid the good doctor. Still, what are we going to do with the rest of the tonic? Guess your friends won't be enjoying it anymore. But you will be, as I am going to mix it up every morning and you will drink it before I leave for work. Do I make myself clear, young lady?" she demanded.

The contrite girl hung her head and answered, "Yes, Ma'am, perfectly."

Of course, she was also thinking about revenge. She would definitely figure out a way to pay back her tattle tale sister and she did.

Every Saturday morning a farmer brought Doris a chicken to cook for Sunday dinner. He put it in a metal crate early in the morning so he could catch her at home to pay him. On Sunday morning, she would ring the bird's neck and pull its head off. Then hang it by the feet on the clothesline with a bucket underneath to catch its blood.

Jenny was scared of live chickens, so the following week Michele had a surprise waiting for her when she returned home at noon on Saturday. At the top of the back stairs, one had to make a right turn onto a landing about three-foot square. On its left side was the building and on the right side was a short cement block wall. This Saturday, Michele crouched behind the wall holding a live chicken by the feet, and her timing was perfect. When Jenny made the turn to step out onto the landing, her willful sister jumped up and put the squawking chicken right in her face.

Jenny screamed, turned around and fled back down the stairs. Lucky for Michele, she didn't rat her out to their mother. Michele thought the chicken tasted better than usual that Sunday. It had the effect she wanted, and Jenny never did that again.

Chapter Four

*W*hen Michele was ten years old Doris married Ed Vane, an event that changed all their lives. Her sister, Jane, was six at the time and thought it would be fun having a daddy again, but Ed didn't turn out to be the kind of new daddy they were looking for. Because the first thing their new dad did, was make them go live with their Uncle June, Aunt Evie, and Cousin Ellen for a year out in the country on a farm. Doris didn't protest his decision so Michele could only assume she agreed.

It wasn't the ideal situation as Uncle June often went into town and returned home, drunk. And if that wasn't bad enough, he would slap Aunt Evie around. Luckily, the young kids could hide upstairs in their bedroom until it was over, afraid he'd decide to slap them around along with their aunt. Sometimes though, Michele would sneak out and look through the banister to see what was happening.

Maybe this was why Aunt Evie wasn't too kind to the kids, like when Jane played around with her food and made Aunt Evie wait to clean up the table. She came up with a new rule, 'the last one to finish eating would get her fingers slapped'. Evidently Aunt Evie wanted to vent her anger out against Uncle June and Michele didn't want Jane to be her victim.

So, Michele decided to take Jane's victim role on herself and deliberately played around with her food longer than Jane did. But it only took Aunt Evie one or two times to catch on, then the control switch was out of Michele's hands.

But she continued to look for a way to control her Aunt's actions and one day she thought she had found it. There was a cat that lived outside, and Michele knew her Aunt liked to hold it sometimes. It was like the Balm of Gilead for her.

As Michele sat looking at the cat, a big rain barrel full of water that sat at the corner of the house also caught her eye and a plan came to mind. She decided to catch the cat and hold its head down in the barrel of water to see how long he could hold his breath. Unfortunately, not as long as she thought, because when she brought his head back up out of the water, it was dead.

A neighbor boy just happened to be running across the property and saw what she did. After he went to the kitchen door and told Aunt Evie what Michele did, she came out and saw Michele standing there with the victim in hand. Michele hung her head in feigned sorrow, but Aunt Evie didn't buy it.

"Aunt Evie, I didn't mean to hurt your cat. I was just playing with it. I'm so sorry."

Her aunt told her, "Go to the barn and get a shovel and then go bury that poor thing in the woods!"

"Are you going to tell Uncle June?" she asked.

Aunt Evie declared, "No, but you will be going to bed without your supper and if Jane is the last one finishing her supper, I will slap her hands. Do I make myself clear?"

Something else different was getting to school. She always walked to school in town but out in the country, they had to ride a school bus. The worst part of riding the bus came during the winter, when she stood at the end of the lane waiting for it. Luckily Jane was half a year too young for school and didn't have to feel the cold. Nor did she have to wear boots and struggle through piles of deep snow that could be a bit dangerous as there might be ice at the bottom of it. Michele and Ellen fell more than once but weren't seriously injured, thank God. One couldn't help wondering if that was how they learned to pray.

Michele didn't like leaving Jane at the mercy of her old aunt, especially if it was on a Monday after a drunken-weekend-episode with Uncle June. Still they didn't seem to have any choices in their lives anymore. The year finally ended, and their stepdad allowed them to live at home again in a part of Ada called Maume. In the Indian language, Maume meant, 'man out of the smoke'. It was a suburb on the northeast side of Ada and on the east side of the Wages River. It was a poor section of town but not as poor as Rossville, where the black folks lived.

The kids were happy to go back home, and to find

during their year away, Ed and Doris had bought a house. They were glad it was actually a house and not another apartment. It had a yard with a garage in the back, along with an outside toilet. Sitting on a cut-out hole in a board was plenty cold in the wintertime. Toilet paper came from catalogs and newspapers. Buckets were used inside during the nighttime. Later on, Ed actually had an addition built onto the house, one which provided a regular toilet and a bathtub.

The house had a front porch too, that was meant to be a place to sit on and enjoy nature. However, the scene in front of the house was hardly enjoyable. Columbus Street ran in front of the house and beyond the street was a dirt levy bank to hold back the river. It had been built after a great flood when the river water rose to an unheard-of height and covered the area of Maume. Still, there was an upside to it. In the summertime, kids could use pieces of cardboard to slide down the hill and in the winter, some fortunate kids had sleds to slide down in the snow. Michele and her poor friends used metal lids from factory barrels. They hammered and bent two opposite sides to use as handles to hold on to.

There was an elementary school that could be seen from the top of the levy directly across the river. It could have been a short walk from their house but unfortunately, in order to reach it, they had to walk north to the top of the levy bank, climb steps up and over the levy, follow a trail a half mile, cross a bridge and then back south for another half mile. The kids walked a mile in the rain or snow to get to a school right across the street. It was on these days, Michele longed for the school bus, which was the only thing she missed, living in the country.

During the winter, the river froze over really good, and the kids were able to take their bikes out to ride on them across it. Sometimes successfully, and other times they had to push them across. Michele wasn't into it much because of the memory of Bob falling through the ice the day he went after Dave.

Also, she didn't have a bike until she got one for her twelfth birthday and Jane managed to mess that up. One day, without permission, Jane took it and went for a ride. When she returned home, she laid it at the curb in front of Ed's car instead of putting it on the front lawn.

Later that day, Ed didn't see it and drove his car over the back wheel. They tried to straighten the wheel again but couldn't. It was so hard to ride, she actually had to pump the pedals going downhill. Jane was punished the usual way by going to bed without any supper.

Chapter Five

The girls received a quarter a week as allowance, but it seemed more like *wages* for doing dishes, making their bed every morning, and general help with the housework. Michele hated doing the toilet and tried to avoid it whenever she could.

Most Saturdays, they were allowed to go into town to watch movies at one of the two theaters and spend their quarter. One theater cost a dime and the other fifteen cents, so they usually chose the cheaper one. Their extra nickels allowed them to buy a bag of popcorn, a drink, and a candy bar that cost a nickel each. Sometimes though, the movie at the more expensive theater was too good to miss so they shared a bag of popcorn and felt satisfied.

At the beginning of fall, in September, things changed as Michele decided to start saving for Christmas gifts. She stopped spending her refreshment money and went without any treats, except the movie itself.

Three months later, with Christmas only two weeks away, like Michele, Jane decided to stop buying anything for herself and gave her extra money to Michele. The following Saturday as Jane gave Michele her extra money, she told her sister, "Now don't forget to put my name on the gifts too."

"Now I know the motive behind your generosity. I've been saving mine for three and a half months. I'll do it for you this time but not next year, and you can count on that!" declared her big sister.

There was an ironic twist to this event when they went to spend time with Bob and Dave a few days before Christmas. The first evening, Michele gave them, along with their dad and stepmother, the gifts she had saved her money to buy. To do this, she denied herself the pleasure of spending any of her allowance on anything, except the movies. She had such a miserably poor life the only way to escape it was to lose herself in the movies, so she felt compelled to go whether right or wrong.

Later that evening after all the kids went to bed, she had to get up to use the bathroom. As she walked quietly down the hall, she overheard a comment that Ella, her malicious stepmother, made to her dad.

"Why in the world would Michele give us handkerchiefs for Christmas? As if we didn't already have enough of them, she brings us more."

"I don't know Ella, but aren't you being a little ungrateful? She and jane can't have much money to buy anything, yet they managed to give all of us a gift. Maybe it is ridiculous in your opinion, but I appreciate them trying" he replied.

Michele sneaked back to bed, feeling another

rejection. "Well, there's always next year and I do have the choice of whether to even give her anything. We'll see!" she thought.

It was the next summer, during the two weeks, that Michele and Jane were allowed to spend with their dad's other family, when Ella showed her true character. The past should have taught Michele that Dave's antics didn't always benefit her, but she followed her brother's lead.

Dave again, got his gullible younger sister in trouble even though it seemed like a good idea, at least in his fourteen-year old mind, and she in her twelve-year old mind thought so too.

A shed near the garden held all of Ella's canning jars that she used to can garden vegetables for use in the winter. Dave wanted to help her with the canning process and thought it would be a nice surprise if he and Michele canned everything that was ripe. So, one day they picked, cut, washed and canned everything they could. They filled quite a few jars which they set back on the shelves in the shed and felt proud of their day's work. They could hardly wait for Ella to get home.

When Ella arrived home later that day after work, she met two excited kids in the driveway. She couldn't imagine what had happened for them to be so excited. But they thought, for once, they had done something that would please Ella.

"Ella, we've got something to show you; a surprise. You're gonna love it". They took her back to the shed and Dave said, "Ok Michele, open the shed doors so she can see!"

Ella stood there with her eyes and mouth wide open. "Oh, my goodness! What have you done?"

"We canned your vegetables, at least the ripe ones, so you wouldn't have too."

"You idiots", she exploded. "Wait till your dad gets home! Now get out of my sight. I'm going to try to save some of this mess you've made."

Dave was devastated! He didn't understand what was wrong with all their hard work. They had wanted to do something nice for their hardworking stepmother, but apparently, she didn't appreciate it. He went inside the house and up to his bedroom where he fell across his bed.

Michele didn't want to be cooped up inside, so she chose to climb up in the big tree located between the driveway and the kitchen door leading into the house.

Finally, after what seemed like a lifetime, Harry drove his truck into a parking space beside the driveway. He went inside to see Ella and waited until it was almost dark, before he came looking for Michele. He walked from the kitchen door over to the big tree where Michele was hiding between two of its big limbs. She thought she was well hidden, but obviously not, because her dad came over, looked up, and said, "You can come down now."

"Are you going to spank me?" she asked.

"No, I think a couple of hours hiding up there in this tree is enough punishment for you. Except like your brother, you'll be going to bed now without any supper," he answered.

The next morning at the breakfast table, Michele whispered to Dave, "Never, and I mean never, am I going to listen to you again!"

This proved to be a false promise, for when she came for her visit the next summer, Dave had found two pairs of boxing gloves and he teased her into sparring with him. She agreed. Maybe it was anger management because her stepfather, who she lived with, was not very nice to anyone in his house, she reasoned.

Still there was one stipulation. Dave had to promise not to hit her in the face, but it seemed he always ended up breaking his promises. Lucky for her, he didn't manage to break her nose or smash her lips.

Then one day, Harry overheard their conversation including Dave's promise. He hid behind the kitchen door and watched the match begin. It didn't take Dave long to break his promise and hit Michele in the face. Harry came out then, grabbed Dave and pulled his arms behind him.

"Ok Michele, now you hit him in the face!" he said.

"Oh boy," she thought, "vengeance is mine!" Unfortunately, when she had the opportunity for revenge, her good character didn't allow her to act for she felt sorry for Dave in his pitiful stance.

"I'm sorry, Dad, I just can't do it!" she said.

So, Harry released Dave's arms saying, "You got lucky this time, but if I ever catch you hitting her in the face again, I'll do the same to you. Do I make myself clear? Apologize to your sister, right now!"

"I'm sorry Sis," he said and must have meant it this time for he never did it again.

Michele sought many ways and looked for things to do, to get away from her new life in Maume. More accurately one could say, from her new dad.

One day she took one of the clothes-line-poles her mother used to prop up the line so the longer heavy clothes like pants, tablecloths and bed coverings wouldn't drag the ground. She used the strings from the meat packages for her line, a rusty washer for a sinker, a piece of tree bark as a bobber, and a safety pin for the hook. There were always plenty of worms on the ground for bait, especially after a rain. She went fishing!

But try as she might she couldn't catch a single fish on her safety pin hook. The only time she even came close, was when she pulled the line in and a fish was holding onto the line. He must not have liked what he was tasting as he spit it out before she could reach him.

Finally, a Good Samaritan named Clyde, came along where she was fishing one morning. "How are you doing? Have you caught anything yet?" he asked.

"No, I can't seem to catch anything, no matter what time of day I try. I wonder maybe if I had a different kind of bait, it'd work?" she asked him.

"Let me see your bait," he replied.

So, Michele took her pole over to him and when he looked at it started to laugh.

"I think I see why! Maybe I can fix your problem," he said. Then reached into his tackle box and brought out a fishhook. He cut her safety pin off and tied the hook to her line. He held up the safety pin and laughingly said;

"This safety pin sure worked for the fish's safety but didn't help you much! Now put a worm on your hook and try it again."

She did, and at the same time he threw his line out. It wasn't but a minute until her bark bobber went sailing out into the water. She was so surprised at it moving, she stood there as if her arms were paralyzed.

"Pull your pole in," he exclaimed. "There's a fish on your hook!"

His voice jarred her mind into action, and she did as he said. She was amazed that she actually caught a fish but knew it was because of the new piece of equipment. It was just a small fish, but none-the-less, Michele felt proud.

"I caught a fish, I caught a fish," she said again in disbelief. When she was settled down from the excitement of catching her first fish, she said;

"It's really small, isn't it? What kind is it?"

"It's a bluegill. They taste good but since they run small, we need to get more to make a meal out of them. If we catch more of them, I'll show you how to clean the fish, so that they are fit to eat. Is that ok with you?" her new friend asked.

"Yeah, let's do it!" she shouted.

Eager now for another fish to bite on her hook, she baited and threw it into the water. Again, and again, she and Clyde pulled the small bluegills from the water.

After they caught quite a few more, he looked around and found a large flat rock to use.

"Now I'm going to show how to clean them. Are you ready?" He asked. Michele was intrigued so she shook her head up and down excitedly.

She felt a little nervous when he reached into his pocket and pulled out a pocketknife but she decided he did show her how to fish so he probably wasn't going to hurt her. Still, she didn't get too close as she watched him slit open the fish's belly to empty out the entrails and then scale the two sides. It made her a bit squeamish when he cut the head, tail and fins off.

He cleaned the rest of the fish and put them in a small burlap sack.

"Do you think your mom would like to fry these up for you and your family? he asked. "I don't need them. I've got plenty more in my icebox at home."

"Oh yeah, I'm sure she will. When my brothers lived with us, she always liked to fix the fish they caught. She'll be grateful to have something different to fix for supper. You could tell how much she was because she always remembered to say grace for them," the smiling girl said to her new friend.

"Ok, here you are," he said handing the sack to her. "I'll catch you later." They parted ways to go home, her up the levy bank and he walked down the shoreline.

"I don't even know his name", she thought. "Guess I'll ask him the next time I see him fishing."

But that never happened since she never saw him again. It seemed their meeting by the water was more than a chance meeting before he disappeared from her life. Reflecting back, she felt he was a gift from God and was thankful. It was a rarity for her in her young life to find a decent man. Most of the men she had known, were definitely not like him.

Chapter Six

*T*he following September Michele began going to her new school, Thompson Elementary, and found she didn't fit, or maybe didn't try to fit in very well. She was a very intelligent girl and frankly became bored. To cover up her boredom she made spit balls and tossed them at other students until the teacher caught her. Her punishment was to stand in the corner, and she spent a lot of time there, sometimes more than at her desk.

One day one of the boys in her class named Pete, mocked her.

"Michele, you think you are so smart. You always give Miss Gigandi the answer she wants!" he said.

"Well, if I had to wait on the rest of you guys, I'd probably fall asleep. Tell you what, I'm challenging you and the rest of your friends to a fight. After school, hang around in the back and when everyone's gone, we'll see how brave and tough you are!" Michele challenged.

He replied, "Ok, fine, we'll meet you there, smarty pants!"

There were five of them when they all met. Pete, their leader, said, "I'm first guys. Let's see if she'll be able to open her mouth or even get up, when I'm done with her."

Then he held up his fists, "Come on pigeon, unless you'd rather apologize right now and turn your scrawny self around and get out of Dodge."

He had barely enough time to shut his mouth before Michele's left fist hit him between his mouth and nose. Then she slammed her right fist hard into his stomach. Next, she kneed him in the groin. He fell to the ground, screaming and holding his private parts and his nose was a mess. His buddies got the message and took off, leaving him to manage getting to his feet alone and hobble away.

Of course, his parents reported her to the principal, Mr. Harvey, who then called Doris. He didn't tell her why he called but just said he needed to speak with her and Michele in his office after school. He also told Miss Gigandi to be there too.

"What's all of this about, young lady?" Doris inquired. "What have you done now?"

"Well Mom, this kid, Pete, challenged me to fight him and his buddies. We met behind the school in the playground. It wasn't my idea and I expected to get the stuffin's beat out of me. But if I didn't show up, I would never live it down. Don't you understand, Mom? I didn't have any other choice. I was scared but I had to do it!"

"Well, now you'll have to face the consequences, I almost feel sorry for you but maybe this'll teach you a lesson you couldn't learn in class no matter how good your teacher is." She replied.

"Mom, Miss Gigandi is really nice and I'm sorry she will probably be involved in this mess too, I hope she understands." Michele answered.

When they arrived at school, Miss Gigandi, along with Pete and his parents, were already waiting with Mr. Harvey. When everyone was seated, Mr. Harvey told Pete to tell him what had happened.

"Well, Sir," Pete said and pointed to Michele. "She told me and my friends to meet her after school let out, back in the playground. When we got there, she walked over to me and started hitting me like some boxer. I was so surprised I couldn't hit her back, anyway. You know us guys aren't supposed to hit girls." He said this as if it came from the Gospel.

Michele was shocked at the liar, but she wasn't a tattletale, so she remained silent.

"So, now that you know the truth! What are you going to do with her, Mr. Harvey?" Pete's father demanded.

He held up his hand, "This is the first time she's gotten into any trouble. Miss Gigandi, do you have any suggestions?" the nervous principal asked.

"Yes, I do have. I think Michele should stay after school every day for one hour. I will have her make up for this. I'm not sure how yet, but I promise you, I will teach her a lesson or two!" the frustrated teacher replied.

"Ok, folks, will this do?" he asked, looking around at the others there.

"Frankly I think she should be suspended!" Pete's

mother huffed. "Me, too," said the father more quietly this time. Years later, Michele figured if Pete's mother ruled the roost, maybe Pete didn't want to follow his parent's lifestyle example and that's why he tried to bully her and others, not wanting to be known as a wimp.

"I'm sorry Ma'am, but this is an elementary school, not a college." Mr. Harvey replied. No one had any other reply, so the meeting ended.

The next day after school let out, Michele stayed at her desk waiting for Miss Gigandi to come back into the room. In a few minutes she returned and asked,

"Now, young lady, what do you think you should do?"

"First of all, I want to apologize for making you stay after school too. I will do whatever I can to make it up to you." responded the sorry student.

"Do you want me to clean up things in here, like papers on the floor?" Michele asked.

"Since that's one of the janitor's jobs, which he gets paid for, we'll let him do that. Let's think of something else you can do, so you can get home before it is a bother to your mother" answered Miss Gigandi.

"It won't be no bother. In fact, Mom didn't tell my stepdad about any of this. I'm glad too, because living with him is hard enough. I can't imagine what kind of punishment he would come up with. You see, Miss Gigandi, he doesn't want me there any way." Michele responded.

"What do you mean?" her teacher asked.

"Well he's told me that my dad didn't want me, nor did he want me in his house!" Michele replied.

"Why in the world would he say a thing like that?" Miss Gigandi asked.

"I don't know; neither does my mom, Miss Gigandi" Michele explained.

"You mean she's heard him say that, or did you just tell her?" Miss Gigandi added.

"I didn't have to tell her, because she's heard him say that lots of times." Michele said. "And he talks mean to her and my little sister, Jane, too. But we don't have anyone else to live with. My Grandma Nora is really old, and needs help herself. She mostly stays in her wheelchair. My older sister, Jenny, lives in the back of her house, kind of like an apartment. She cooks and cleans for Grandma and I'm sure glad she does."

"Of course, she doesn't have to pay any kind of rent, so it works out for both of them. Plus, I'm sure Jenny's husband appreciates it too. I don't know how she's gonna keep doing it though, because she's going to have a baby real soon. So, you see why I can't leave home, even though I'd sure like to."

"Oh, yeah I forgot. There's my Uncle June, which my stepdad paid to let me, and Jane stay with last year for a whole year, when he and my mom first got married. He is a mean old man and we sure wouldn't want to live out there on his farm again, no way." Michele explained even further.

"Well Michele, you've not had a very good life so far, so let's try to make it better. You are very intelligent and creative so let's put those abilities into something fun that will make time fly. And, yes, you are a very special young lady and I am glad to be your teacher!" her teacher affirmed to her.

"Do you really mean that, Miss Gigandi? I know sometimes I cause trouble, like when I got in a fight with Pete. But you have to understand, he and a lot of the kids don't like me, and they make fun of me. Even the girls say things to and about me that aren't nice, like when I always hold up my hand when you ask us for an answer to a question. I only hold it up after you wait for a while and no one else answers and because I feel kind of bad for you, standing up there and waiting. Then one day, Sally, leaned over and whispered, 'Of course you know the answer, Miss Smarty Pants!'"

"Ok, I see, Michele, and let me say 'thank you' because sometimes I don't feel very much like a teacher. So, I want you to do whatever you'd like. You may even leave now and go on home but try to think of something we can do tomorrow, ok?" her teacher asked.

"Yes Ma'am, and thank you so much, I'll try very hard to make you proud of me!" was her response.

That was the beginning of a better relationship with Miss Gigandi, but unfortunately her home life didn't improve, and for the most part, the next three years, she still felt unloved and unwanted.

Chapter Seven

Michele missed her brothers who always led her into doing things, ironically it was Dave, who always seemed to get her into some kind of trouble. But Dave wasn't in her home now, it was just Michele and Jane, who was too young to do very much with except go to the movies. Michele started looking for other ways than going to the movie house to enrich her life. Although going to the movies may have been what gave her the idea to start a gang with the local boys.

Tony was her first recruit to the new gang, then Fred and his brother Dan joined. Next Chuck and his cousin Mark wanted to join.

As the leader, Michele came up with a new game to challenge the boys. At the northwest end of town there was a deserted factory. In fact, several old buildings sat side by side but the one which had the most windows was her first choice. The game was to see who could throw a rock and break the highest window and then who could break the most of them. They each took turns and had the privilege of choosing the stones they were going to throw.

Each one had to chip in two nickels that she held until the games were over, then five nickels went to the best shot in each category. Of course, as their leader she chose the order for them to perform and always rotated the order so no one could complain; at least about that.

Michele had a talent for winning, or one might say, a determination to outdo her followers which is probably why she was the leader. Of course, being intelligent and artistic helped. Also being deserted by her dad and mistreated by her stepdad might have made her something of a young controller.

She taught the gang to be creative as they used chalk to write and draw on anything they chose, houses, buildings, even the sidewalks were a canvas. Unfortunately, there was not any financial gain in that adventure. But there was 'old satisfaction,' especially when being creative meant getting back at some unlikable people.

When something more than chalk drawings was needed for that 'old satisfaction', finding eggs came in handy. Local people who raised chickens provided them with eggs to use as decorations for their contempt.

Probably the best fun they had was tipping over outhouse-toilets that were plentiful in their neighborhood.

Halloween was the special time her gang pulled this latest prank. Since their families were basically poor, store bought costumes were hardly ever seen. But they could improvise some old clothes for some kind of a costume, paint up their faces, take grocery sacks, paint cans or buckets and gather candy that wasn't a regular treat. Some of them even got money, the best treat of all, if it amounted to enough.

Most of the residents got a big kick out of this night and were generous in their giving except for one of them. A crabby and unfriendly old man who lived by himself wouldn't take part in this usual fun night for the community. He wouldn't even open his door to the kids let alone give them any treats.

Well, Michele thought her gang should bring some justice into town, after all wasn't that what heroes did? Anyway, this Halloween night she told her new gang to meet her back of her garage around ten o'clock, after their parents and everyone else would have gone to bed.

When they all showed up, she told them her plan of justice with the old man.

"Tony, I want you to go to edge of town where a man raises horses. Sneak into the stables and collect as much manure as you can get in this grocery bag then bring it back here within the next hour."

"Fred and Dan go to the property where chickens rule the roost, at least it sounds like they do from all their squawking, and they bring back all the eggs you can find. Be back in an hour like Tony."

"Chuck and Mark, you'll have to hurry, I want you to go out a bit farther to a farm and bring back two buckets full of cow manure, and everyone be back within the hour."

"I will go over the levy bank and bring back all the wet, stinking mud I can put in these two big paint cans that I collected just for this occasion."

Of course, she was the first one back and waited for the rest of her gang to return. She was so excited that setting still wasn't possible. She paced back and forth, wondering how everything was going for the team and just how much longer they were going to be. She could hardly wait!

Finally, after what seemed a lifetime, they all met again behind her garage and Michele told them the plan. Fred and Dan were to go first and sneak up onto the crabby man's front porch then quietly break the eggs all over it. Next Tony was to lean over the banister and pitch the horse manure over the porch floor. Next Chuck and Mark were to do the same with the cow manure.

When they were finished, she said, "Go get some water and mix it up with the rest of your payback donations like I've already done."

It only took them a short time to get their buckets of water from a pump in a neighbor's well and gather around Michele again.

"Now watch and do what I do," she said and took her paint cans of watery mud to the porch. She emptied them out by throwing the contents against the door and window screens. They followed suit with more cans of water then went across the next neighbor's yard and hid among the big bushes. That is, all except Michele who took a handful of gravel and threw it at his bedroom window making a terrible racket till his bedroom light came on.

Then she joined her conspirators and watched as the front room light came on. The front door opened and out came the crabby old man who slipped on all the mess waiting for him on the porch floor. He fell down yelling and cursing but luckily nothing seemed to be broken as he stomped back inside.

The next morning, he called the police and reported what happened to him, so they came out to his house to see the damages. Then they went around the neighborhood asking if anyone had seen anything. Of course, no one had seen anything, nor did anyone really care because the man was not someone you'd choose for a neighbor or a friend.

Her stepfather questioned Michele about the incident who appeared perfectly innocent of any wrongdoing. But nasty old Ed could have been a friend to old Crabby since their dispositions were similar.

"I don't have a clue to what you're talking about," Michele told him and then said a silent prayer to her true father, God, and asked for forgiveness.

After the questioning was over, she went around and gathered her gang together then went up on the levy bank where they could be alone. They talked about what was going on with the police searching for the culprits and Michele told them that they needed to retaliate.

"You mean again, with the police snooping around! What do you want to do this time?" Tony asked.

"Well Ole' Crabby didn't seem to get our message so we have to send him another one and I think I've got an answer," she said.

"Really, maybe we should lay back for a while, what do you other guys think?" Tony asked.

"I don't know, but whatever you all think, I'm in," volunteered Chuck. "Me, too," said Mark.

"Ok, if everyone else wants to count me in too," Tony conceded.

"Ok, is anyone against it?" Michele inquired.

No one was, so she said, "Here's the plan. Tonight, after dark meet me behind my garage. When you're all here we're going to sneak over to the back of Crabby's house and push his outhouse over. That's the best thing I can think of. Do any of you guys have a better idea?" No one answered. "Ok, I'll see you tonight."

They all met again behind her garage shortly after dark. "Ok, let's go, guys, but remember, keep quiet in case anybody's up."

They sneaked down the alley to the back yard of his house and she signaled with her hand to come on to the front of the outhouse then whispered, "Ok, on the count of three, push it over. One, two three."

The outhouse went backwards but its door flew open and to everyone's, and I mean everyone's surprise, there stood old Crabby with his overalls down around his ankles which he was trying to pull up. Everybody screamed or yelled, and it would have been impossible to determine who was the most surprised, embarrassed or afraid.

But the kids did the smart thing when they turned around and hightailed it out of there.

They ended up together where they started out, behind Michele's garage.

"Oh, boy, what do we do now? Will he call the police and report us?" asked Tony.

"Hey calm down! It's our word against his. Let me think a minute!" ordered their leader. So, they waited.

"Ok, there's really nothing we can do. Go on home and let's see what happens tomorrow. It could have been worse!" Michele stated.

"How could it have been any worse?" asked Fred.

"Well, he could have stepped backwards into the hole in the ground, into the poo!" Michele exclaimed.

"Go on home and get some sleep, we'll meet again here about noon, by then we'll probably know how it's going to go, or at least have some idea."

"Yeah, if we're not all in jail!" declared Dan.

They all met the next day and every single one of them were in a state of amazement because none of them had heard anything from anyone!

"Well guys, I guess no news is good news. Maybe Ole' Crabby is too embarrassed to do anything about it. He probably wouldn't appreciate it if everyone heard about his outhouse adventure," reasoned Michele.

"Hey, I sure wouldn't say anything either if I was in his shoes or caught with my pants down!" snickered Tony. All of them laughed out of mutual embarrassment or relief, probably both.

The following week revealed Crabby's intentions about their pranks, one of the local realtor's had posted a 'For Sale' sign in the yard. The price must have been remarkably low because within a few days the sign was gone along with the old man.

The next thing Michele decided they needed to do was give their gang a name and she had one in mind,

The Maume Elite. She got in touch with them and called a meeting that evening, the usual time, after dark, the usual place, behind her garage.

When they were gathered, she told them her idea of naming their gang, The Maume Elite!

"Well, maybe you better tell us what the word elite means, and then we can vote on it," Tony suggested.

Michele pulled out a piece of paper to read from. "According to the dictionary, she said, elite means, 'the group or part of a group selected or regarded as the finest, best, most distinguished, most powerful,' and I believe that sounds just like our team," Michele informed them.

"I think that fits us to a T. Are the rest of you guys in agreement?" Tony asked.

They all yelled "Yeah!" And it was settled. The vote was unanimous.

What they didn't know was they were on their way to stardom, of a sort.

Chapter Eight

*I*ndependence Day meant a lot to the townspeople, and to say they celebrated it with a big bang, was an understatement. Actually, they did celebrate with a bang as there was a huge Civil War cannon used to make the biggest bang. It set in an area where the main bridge came over the Wages River connecting Ada with Maume. Each year the mayor, city council and other bigwigs of town, along with a writer and photographer of the Ada Daily News, were all there. As many of the town's people that could fit in the area, met there to hear the mayor speak and show their loyalty to America.

The day before the meeting was to take place, one of the city workers readied the cannon with a small amount of gun powder stuffed down deep in the barrel. At the rear end of the barrel on top, was a hole for a fuse and several pieces of string were twisted together to form the fuse that would ignite the powder. The mayor would signal the worker to light it as the high school band played the National Anthem. When the powder was lit, it produced a loud noise but only a small bit of smoke would come out of the cannon's barrel.

This year the celebration would be different. The ones who were most eagerly awaiting this Independence Day's big bang were the Maume Elite.

The night before, 'the gang' was very busy collecting eggs, horse and cow manure, with a bit of mud just as the year before. But it wasn't a payback day this time, just one of mischievousness and maybe just plain boredom with life.

Anyway, they took their collections and a long clothesline pole to stuff the cannon barrel. After the deed was done, they could hardly wait until the next afternoon celebration when the powder in the canon was lit. They hoped they'd truly have reason to celebrate, in fact more than anyone else could ever imagine.

The next day all the celebrities of Ada and loads of common people were gathered around in the area. The mayor, as usual, used the opportunity to let the people know how lucky they were to have him as their public servant. He stood just a short distance from the opening of the barrel for the greatest effect of his Independence Day speech.

Finally, the band started playing and the mayor signaled his helper to light the fuse. There were the usual few seconds of anticipation before the loud boom, when everyone stood with expectancy. Then came the big bang and along with it out came the 'surprise of the day'. It covered the mayor from head to toe as well as all the others standing near him. What a mess! Even the photographer was so surprised he didn't even think to do his job. That may have been a blessing for him because any pictures would probably have cost him his job along with his reputation.

After the gang saw what happened, they took off down the levy bank away from all the noise and chaos, laughing their way homeward. Because of all the confusion and mess, their leaving went unnoticed. They met behind the garage where everyone kept talking and laughing. Still Michele was finally able to calm them down.

"Hey, guys, I'm calling this meeting to some kind of order!" Michele screamed. She sat down on an overturned bucket and told them to all sit down on the ground and be quiet. They sat down but were still out of control for the next few minutes. Finally, they all managed to be quiet long enough for the leader to say,

"Listen up gang, what do you think is next. I can't imagine how we'll ever, and I mean ever, top this one!"

Nor could anyone else, so they all split up to go home and hide out in case any of their families wondered where they were at the celebration.

The next day, thanks to the Ada Daily reporter, they became famous as everybody in town was talking and reading about them.

The headlines said, 'Local Vandals Ruin the Celebration.' The town and the ones who lived nearby were telling their communities all about it over the radio stations.

The third day after the incident, Michele called a meeting and started it by asking,

"Well guys, what do you think about all our fame? Does anybody have any answers, I'm all ears!"

After a few moments of silence, Tony replied, "I'm afraid someone will figure out that we were the culprits and we'll be in a heap of trouble so why don't we just not meet again for a while, what do the rest of you guys think?"

"Good idea because my folks are already asking me if I know anything about this," said Dan.

"Does everyone agree?" Their leader asked.

The boys all seemed to be in agreement, as no one ventured any more comments, so Michele said,

"Ok, this meeting is adjourned!" Sadly, or not, they never met again. Probably because the boys were scared and after all Michele did have her moment of glory.

Three years passed with no more gang activities. The summer Michele turned seventeen, she got her first job. The local grocery store, in downtown Ada, hired her part time to work in the meat department, weighing and wrapping packages of meat for the customers.

Nothing was prepackaged; all the meat was cut or ground fresh. She worked with the meat, bare handed; plastic gloves weren't required in those days. She simply greeted each customer, asking them what kind and how much meat they wanted. Then she opened the sliding glass door, reached into the display case and brought out the meat they wanted.

A scale set on top of the case to weigh the amount they wanted, then she wrapped it in a piece of heavy white paper. A string was wrapped around the paper and the price was marked on the package.

Frankly, she thought it was kind of boring and spent most of her time watching the help and customers go by or as they went up and down the aisles.

One woman she nicknamed "The cash register watcher," was a grumpy, sour-faced old lady. Either she'd had a bad life or was having a bad day. Michele thought she could add, 'having a 'bad hair day' to her list since she didn't have much of it or didn't know what to do with the small amount she had.

Anyway, she came up to the meat counter and looked at Michele or maybe one should say, frowned at her. Michele was told to be courteous, smile and speak pleasantly to all customers. So, being younger, and following instructions, she didn't return the ladies frown. Instead she asked, "May I help you?" The question came with as much enthusiasm as when she asked her mother if she could wash the dishes for her.

But what an optimist she was at age seventeen. Years later, she would be able to relate to that old person every time she looked into a mirror. The frowning face she saw, sometimes made her wonder who that old lady was looking back at her.

Still, that day she couldn't help wondering if the old lady ever looked into a mirror; as many times as she had waited on her, she never ever saw her smile one time.

And to tell the truth, Michele too was having a bad day. Her boyfriend had dumped her the night before and said she was too strait-laced, not as in a corset either.

She did wear a waist cincher when she dressed up for special occasions but necking in his car wasn't one of them. So, the last person she needed to deal with that day was this old witch. She was tempted, in fact, and almost offered the lady the broom standing beside the backdoor. She thought the lady could get on it and fly away from her, taking that negative attitude out of her brain length. Or worse yet, have her burned at the stake!

But of course, that didn't happen. Instead, the lady just stood there and demanded one quarter pound of dried beef. As Michele brought out the dried beef it reminded her of the old lady's wrinkled skin.

Michele put what she thought would be the correct amount on the scale, but it was a bit over, so she reached and picked up what she thought was needed to get the perfect weight. But then instead of putting the extra meat back into the case, she threw it into her mouth. That shocked the old lady, and then she shocked Michele by saying with an uplifted nose, "Well, if everyone is going to eat out of there, I don't want it!"

Michele replied, "Suit yourself."

The customer stomped off and left the store. She was a little concerned the lady would stop off at the manager's office and report her. But, she didn't, or maybe she did, and her boss didn't appreciate her small business, so he didn't fire her.

Michele didn't know where the lady flew off to. She never saw her again and later checked to see if her broom was still by the backdoor. The piece of dried beef turned out to be the best dried beef she'd ever tasted.

Chapter Nine

It was 1952 when Michele started her final year as a senior in Ada High School. She had advanced so far in her class subjects she only went to school in the morning. That turned out to be good for her as she obtained a job as a telephone operator, working every afternoon and on Saturdays.

She would have loved to further her education by going to a college but unfortunately there weren't any scholarships available and no one in her family could pay the tuition. There was just no way for her to attend college that she knew about, such as student loans. Thus, the following year she continued her job as a telephone operator.

For an active young person like Michele the job was very boring, and she had to fight the boredom by looking for ways to stay awake. Her job as an operator was to answer the light with a "What number would you like?"

Then take the wire and plug it into the given number, unless it was already lit up showing someone was talking on it. When that happened, she'd say,

"I'm sorry, but that number is busy."

Eavesdropping on people's calls was the best way to find some interest in her work but she could have lost her job. She heard a lot of information, sometimes corny or amusing, even sad. But on one of those eavesdropping calls, she heard a man trying to entice a young woman to let him come over and spend the night with her.

"Your parents are on a two-day vacation trip, who's going to know?" He asked convincingly.

The young girl was stammering, uncertain about what to say or do but Michele knew, and said,

"Don't listen to that stuff, he's trying to get you to do something you'll be sorry for later!"

"What! Who are you?" he yelled.

"Nobody you'd care to meet," she answered authoritatively, "or my two older brothers! Or maybe you'd like me to report you to the juvenile authorities!" challenging him.

He chickened out and slammed the telephone back into its holder. But the young and gullible girl was still on the telephone and said,

"I don't know who you are or what to say but please don't tell anyone about this."

Michele had to add, "Listen kid and learn something from this. Growing up is not very easy, in fact you'll probably make a lot of mistakes but keep yourself pure till you get married and hopefully you'll find a husband who will honor you for this."

"Do you know how to pray?" Michele inquired.

"Yes, yes, my dad's a preacher," she returned.

Michele began, "I'm praying for you right now and maybe I'm kinda like your savior tonight, but don't confuse me with being your Holy Savior. I don't know much about him since I've never gone to church."

Not meaning to, Michele made that confession to her. Ironically, her Grandma Nora always confessed to a priest until she married a divorced man and the Catholic Church excommunicated her. Due to that, Doris never went to church or taught her kids that they should go.

The young girl said, "Thank you so much," and hung up her phone.

Michele just shook her head realizing that while she had performed a good service it was not one that she was getting paid for. She was lucky the incident didn't turn out bad and cause her to lose her job. Then, her humorous nature from being born on April fool's day kicked in. She recalled how people had always played tricks on her. As a kid she didn't like being born on April fool's day but later found that laughter is the best medicine and felt blessed to have been born on that day. Now, maybe God would turn all the tricks of her past life into future blessings......

*Dedicated to my sister-in-law
Carolyn:*

Carolyn

'A New Reunion'

Chapter One

Amazon Rain Forest

God is amazing in how He works and rewards His faithful ones. The following story is a good example.

"Wouldn't it be nice to have a family reunion?" Bob, the oldest family member, posed the question to his sister Michele. He had left his home in California to visit his sister back in Ohio.

"If we wait much longer, I won't be here to enjoy getting to see everyone again."

"I rode them trains so many years, I lost track of my family. It was only by chance I run into Billy and Katie bumming my last train ride."

"Then again, maybe it wasn't just by chance. Maybe God had me take that one last ride to meet up with two run-away kids and give them a home."

"At first, I had no way knowing they were any kin to me but the longer I listened to them talk the more I realized who they were."

"They lived with me a few years but when they were

grown, they both took off again, I guess we all must have a roaming spirit in us."

They sat in silence a few minutes reflecting on their lives, each had regrets but then most people do. Bob always wanted a wife and kids of his own, and a place to call home but somehow the train whistle kept calling him to come ride! He finally had all these things but a wife when his uncle left him his farm and then he run into Billy and Katie. They lived with him the next five years then were gone again.

As long as Michele could remember, she had looked for a man's love. She wanted her dad's love, but he didn't give it to her, nor did her stepdad.

All she had were her brothers, half-brothers and sisters, children and stepchildren, who provided her with more than enough siblings to love and care for when her marriages failed.

"I've been thinking about the same thing ever since you come to see me," Michele responded.

Suddenly she was back to Bob's question but didn't have a clue how to go about finding family members she'd lost contact with over thirty years ago.

"But how do you purpose finding everyone? she asked. "I know Anne is somewhere in South America at a missionary camp. It's in the Amazon Rain Forest and my sister-in-law Carolyn is the camp director. I'm sure I have the address somewhere, maybe we could contact her."

"That's a great idea", Bob agreed. "It's a start."

"But I have no idea where Billy or Katie are, it's

been years since I heard a word from either of them. And Terry Lee, I wonder where his wandering has taken him?" Michele pondered the thought, "I'll have to ask his mother, Jean, where he is."

Since nothing was planned for the day, Michele went to a closet and pulled out a box containing old pictures and papers.

"I'm sure it's here someplace," she said to no one in particular. Since all her kids were grown and gone from her care, she had adopted Goldenrod, a yellow and white cat. Often, she talked to him but not expecting to get an answer. Lost in her thoughts about the missionary camp address she momentarily forgot Bob was listening until she heard his voice.

"What's that you say there Michele? My hearing isn't as good as it used to be?"

"I was just talking to myself", she replied. "I do that sometimes when there is no one else here."

"I was just thinking how amazing God is and how he works and rewards people who are faithful to Him. Isaiah, the prophet, must have felt amazed at the awesomeness of God when he penned the words found in Chapter 55:8-9 that says;

'My thoughts are not your thoughts, neither are your ways My ways, says the Lord. For as the heavens are higher than the earth, so are my ways higher than your ways, and My thoughts than your thoughts.'"

After an hour of searching thru the box Michele suddenly said, "Here it is Bob, I knew I put Carolyn's last post card in this box if I could just find it again."

"You know something Bob, I just remembered hearing about a short-term mission's trip to South America and they were asking for volunteers to work."

"Would you want to volunteer? I'll go with you. Maybe we could see Carolyn, and Anne. Oh, Bob I do so miss seeing my Anne."

The next day Michele mailed a letter to Carolyn asking about the camp and who all was there. Little did she or Bob know, until a month later when she received Carolyn's letter, that Terry Lee and then Billy had just arrived at the missionary camp she directed. She said a letter didn't have nearly enough room to tell how they all got there but they would be tickled to death to have her and Bob come down and spend some time.

Carolyn said, "The mission's buildings were quaint but adequate, located deep in the Amazon Rain Forest". Michele was afraid she knew what Carolyn meant by adequate as she had been there before as a kid.

"There is a small church built by the locals and visionary missionaries. Of course, the construction was done by carpenters who were willing to travel great distances and bring battery driven tools. There isn't any electricity available, so we needed the electricians and plumbers to bring their battery driven tools. Unfortunately, the batteries don't last forever, and they too became waste thrown into the rivers and forest."

"It was the same forest that provided the trees to build the buildings, but then the forest seemed endless. Others brought roofing and glass materials as well as other small items such as ropes, strings, nails, screws, and hinges that might be needed. In fact, most were delivered right to their doorstep like the milkman used to put the milk on the consumer's doorstep."

"It is an everchanging recluse for worldwide missionaries, local and surrounding tribes as well as tourists of all ages. The majority of adults are Christians, but some are of other religions, even those who don't believe in anything or anyone also come just out of curiosity. Then there are reporters, writers, and entrepreneurs who come just to learn how they can use the camp simply to make money."

"Not many poor people come, except locals, as it costs money to get here. Also, not many like the housing facilities as they have to sleep in tents or in sleeping bags. Food is cooked over wood campfires and even worse they have to bathe in the river."

"For social gatherings, sometimes, if it is raining (which happens a lot), we are allowed to use a kitchen located in the back of the church building. There is plenty of water and we can even heat food over great big candles. One can image how canned food, especially soup, is very popular."

"Beside the kitchen is a bedroom for the presiding minister and both rooms plus the sanctuary are lighted by oil filled lanterns. Some of the campers also use the lanterns for lighting.

"Everyone washes their clothes in the same river, most at a narrow spot where rocks can be used to beat their clothing clean. Beating helps clean their clothes as well as to get the water out before being hung on ropes tied between the nearest trees to finish drying."

"It's like going to the local laundry mat. You don't have to walk very far carrying heavy wet clothes and the air makes them smell good. We do have a small problem with the monkeys as they like the smell of clean clothes too and come to mark and reclaim their territory."

"Hope to see you soon, I won't tell the others you might be coming and let it be a surprise."

Love Carolyn

Chapter Two

Mail didn't reach the missionary camp daily, even weekly. Once a month all deliveries were brought downstream to the camp by boat from the nearest town. And any out-going mail was taken on the boat's return trip a month later. Carolyn's letter to Michele didn't leave until the boat came again the next month and it wasn't until another month that the boat brought Michele's letter saying she and Bob would be coming in September. She could hardly wait to see Michele and have her see her daughter Anne, here at the mission's camp.

During the wait there had already been one surprise when Katie saw her mother Anne. Terry Lee, Billy and Katie had all come in one by one. Excitement was mounting for Carolyn as she thought about how their family had been scattered so many years and now was about to come together again.

When it finally got to be September, Carolyn started watching for the boat to come any day. She knew it would have to make a special trip to carry the belongings of the mission's work team but didn't know the exact date of arrival.

Finally, they came and what a reunion they had. After years of separation they couldn't stop talking and hugging one another.

Then on Sunday afternoon, the missionaries met together and since the weather was good, they sat outdoors around a non-burning fire ring forming a circle. The first thing they discussed was that morning's attendance, their actions and reactions to the message that Pastor Jim preached. There wasn't much feedback from the congregation, but the missionaries all agreed it was a great sermon. Jim was pleased. They all took turns preaching on Sunday morning and that day it had been his turn.

Then the conversation took on a rather carefree tone as different ones started sharing their past lives. The first one to speak, was probably also the youngest. It was Katie. She told them what a privilege it was to be there and even though she'd only been with them a week, she felt so welcome, almost like it was home and then, looking around at each of them, said, "It's almost like our family is having a reunion here." Little did she know, for Carolyn hadn't shared Michele's letter with the others.

The next one to speak was Terry Lee, who said, "Well, young lady, I haven't been here much longer, but I agree with you one hundred percent. Some of my pastor friends who have been here before, pretty much said the same thing. Then of course, those of us here are all a part of God's family. After my reclusive past, I came here hoping to find people I could help."

Carolyn said, "That's a good idea but remember this is the Lord's Day to rest and worship. Maybe tomorrow we could go into the nearest village and see who we can find that needs our help. They are, without a doubt, some of the neediest people I've ever had the privilege to tell about our heavenly father and the great future available if they'd just believe in Jesus Christ. But life has been so hard for them, especially the ones who've inherited that dreadful disease, AIDS. It's almost like leprosy. People tend to shun them even if they're not purposely trying to spread AIDS."

"Yes, but God has blessed them in another way", responded Anne. "This camp is a haven for those starving souls. Thanks to all of you who work here and everyone who provides the funds to buy food and the means to bring it out here in the middle of nowhere."

"When I think of all the money the world wastes on people who aren't in need, it makes me sad. In fact, our home country of America, is probably the worst at worshipping and idolizing sports and movie stars."

"Then there's the old expression, 'keeping up with the Jones.' Everyone wants bigger houses, new cars, boats, you name it. And what about the medical and educational cost? As I have said so many times, I believe medical costs should be free. Not only are they not free but unreasonably expensive. People are dying in our country because they can't afford cancer treatment. One chemo bag can cost ten thousand dollars, one bag!"

"You know what makes me sad?" interjected Bob. "And believe me Billy, at my age, I've seen a lot. Just in my lifetime, abortion was legalized in America while American couples are paying thousands of dollars to adopt babies, even from other countries."

"What's so hopeless", Pastor Jim said, "is how the political groups are trying to take God out of everything. First out of our schools, and then if that wasn't enough passing a law to prohibit posting the Ten Commandments in public buildings." He shook his head.

"But there's hope! We Christians, although fewest in number in the world, have the greatest power living within us, the Holy Spirit. Unfortunately, few of us use Him."

"I don't mean to interrupt you guys, but I'm interested in finding out about everyone's past, good and bad, so I'll start with mine, ok?" Katie said.

"Yes, sure, that's sounds like a good idea," interjected Terry Lee.

Katie began, "Well by the time I was almost thirteen, I had read stories about the railroad bums and actually envied their freedom. So, I cut my hair off short, filled a bag with food, a blanket, and a few clothes and went down to the local railroad track. I waited for the next train to stop that had doors open on the side hidden from the station. I saw some men reach up and partially slide a door open then climb in, so I decided to do the same in another car. Fortunately, I wasn't too short to get into the car by myself. Later there was a grey-haired old man and a kid about my age who climbed in. In fact, they were Bob and Billy," Katie declared.

"Well long-lost adopted child, it's good to see you again", Bob declared. "When you turned eighteen, you went off on your own and I never heard from you again. What happened to you?"

"I'm so sorry I did that to you Bob", Katie answered. I was kind of lost and ended up in a shelter for the homeless. I decided I needed help, and the only one available was a local minister who visited the shelter on a weekly basis. What I didn't know was that God had a plan for the rest of my life. He revealed Himself to me when I accepted his Son as my Savior. After that, I began praying and studying the Bible. I grew in my faith and wanted to give back to Him. I found a local church and discovered the need for missionaries and volunteered to become one. I was trained to serve Him and here I am today, knowing He has led me to whoever He wanted me to talk to."

A short time of silence followed her testimony. And then another piece of the puzzle was revealed when Anne spoke up.

"Katie Vincent, do you know who I am?"

Katie quickly answered, "Yes Mother, I know who you are! Please forgive me. I know it isn't any excuse but after you moved us back to Ohio, I felt you would be better off if I wasn't in your life, so I ran off on a train." She hung her head and tears flowed freely down her cheeks.

"O my, Michele, I just realized you are my half-sister from Ada, Ohio?" Billy moaned.

"Yes, I am. Come here and let me hug you," pleaded Michelle.

"I ran away too!" Billie went on, "just like Katie and Bob, but I never forgot my half-sister and how good you were to me even though my father was very cruel to you. Mom couldn't handle him and our lives, so I ran away."

"Michele, have you seen my mom lately", Terry asked? Truth be told, I haven't been in touch with her in a long time."

Michele answered, "Yes, I did! Bob and I went to visit Jean before we came here."

"Auntie, I'll write her a letter you can take with you when you go home," Terry promised.

"I guess we're cousins then, or something, Terry Lee!" Billy declared. "Do you guys realize that not only are we family here, but will also be family in Heaven? How wonderful is that!"

They had a shouting good time praising the Lord and cried with great joy as they gathered in a circle hugging each other, a blessed and united family!

Printed in the United States
By Bookmasters